To...

With many holy wishes from

E. Gaesché S.J.

Retreat of 131

MIRRORS OF GOD

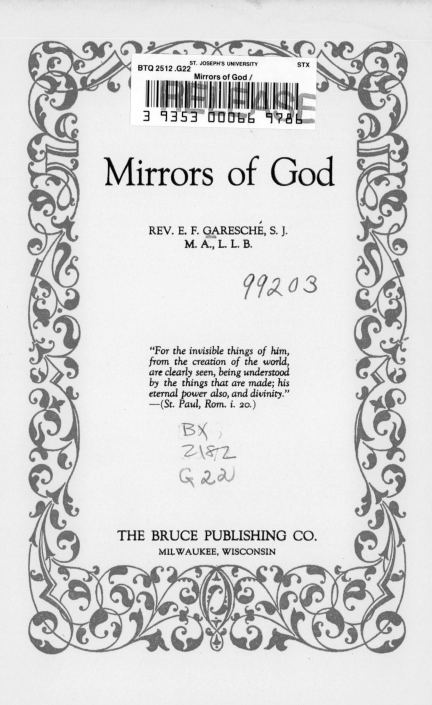

Mirrors of God

REV. E. F. GARESCHÉ, S. J.
M. A., L. L. B.

99203

"*For the invisible things of him,
from the creation of the world,
are clearly seen, being understood
by the things that are made; his
eternal power also, and divinity.*"
—(St. Paul, Rom. i. 20.)

BX
2182
G22

THE BRUCE PUBLISHING CO.
MILWAUKEE, WISCONSIN

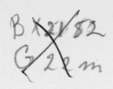

Imprimi potest
MATTHEW GERMING, S. J.
Praepositus Provinciae Missourianae
Nihil Obstat
HENRY B. RIES
Censor Librorum
Imprimatur
✝ S. G. MESSMER
Archiepiscopus Milwauchiensis
March 12, 1927

DEDICATION

To Christ, the King of Kings, and to His Virgin Mother, the Mirror of Justice, I offer this little book on So Great a Theme, So Dear to Their Hearts.

PREFACE

THE DEAR St. Teresa of Avila, who knew so well the hidden depths of friendship with God, once declared, "It is no wonder that it is hard for us to become friends with God, because His nature is so different from our own." Indeed, though our minds were made to know God and our hearts to love Him, we must labor and toil to learn of His beauty and must discipline our hearts lest the love of creatures which we see should lure us away from the love of the Uncreated Whom we do not see.

Yet, the one end of our being is to know God and to love Him. The greatest merit of our humanity comes from loving Him with a pure and simple love. All else is as nothing in comparison with this sublime achievement; and the whole universe besides ourselves, nay, our own bodies and souls, were all created so as to aid us to love God more.

It is the purpose of this book, which is a series of contemplations on the love of God, to help us to discern the lineaments of God's beauty and lovableness from the dim mirrors of creatures, each of which reflects in its own way something of the perfections of its Creator. The earth and the heavens with all their array, the stars, the sea, the skies, the flowers, the races of men, human history, the marvels of science, the heroism of great souls, all these aid us to conceive the goodness and lovableness of God, and to fan the flames of our love of Him by the contemplation of His wonderful works.

May the message of this little book bring to many souls the most precious gift of a greater love of God, and may those who find in its pages some inspirations to that love, breathe a prayer for all the rest who read it and for the author thereof, that all may be kindled to the greater love of God for His own sake, because He is so good in Himself and so worthy to be loved above all things.

The Feast of the Assumption.

TABLE OF CONTENTS

Pages

Preface 7-8

CHAPTER I

GOD'S LOVABLENESS—The Tendrils of the Heart—Prone
on the Earth—The Craving for God—Why Is It Hard to
Love?—The Ways of Knowledge—For Our Merit—The
Need of Effort—The Book of Love 11-20

CHAPTER II

THE MIRROR OF MEN—When Light Departs—The Mirrors
of Creation—Clearer and Clearer—The Sentient World—
The Sea Gulls—Creation's Chasm—The Intelligence of
Man—God's Image in Our Spirit—The Creative Imagination—Man's Godlike Will—Jewish and Christian Heroes ... 21-34

CHAPTER III

THE MIRROR OF THE STARS—"Lift Up Your Hearts!"—
Neglect--Uncouth and Barbarous—The Sky's Vast Abysses—
The Unchanging Starry Scenery—The Universe of Stars—
A Cry of Love—"For Your Own Sake" 35-45

CHAPTER IV

THE MIRROR OF HISTORY—Down the Corridors of His-
tory—New Reasons to Love God—The Pageant of History—
The Toil of Aeons—The Upholding of the Universe—The
Daybreak of History—Man's Primitive Outwanderings—Old
Tombs of Oldest Kings—The Torrential Nations 46-56

CHAPTER V

THE MIRROR OF SCIENCE—The Trumpet-Tone of Paul—
Science—the Handmaid of Love—The Darkness of Hearts—
Forms of Loveliness—Universes in Miniature—The Marvels
of Plants—The Rich Harvest of Science—Our Human
Microcosm—Health's Delicate Balances—The Healing Power
—The Litany of Science—Our Little Store of Learning 57-71

CHAPTER VI

THE MIRROR OF FLOWERS—In the Sweet Forests—The
Tribe of Lilies—The Meaning of Flowers—Flowers--God's
Thoughts—The Year's Processional—In Varying Climes—
The Alpine Bloom—Blossoms of Ocean—The Rose of the
Blessed 72-82

Pages

CHAPTER VII

THE MIRROR OF GREAT SOULS—Differences of Resemblance—A Salutary Thought—Delusive Self-Sufficiency—The Splendor of Genius—Great Souls of Science—The Sagacity of Rulers—Great Myths and Histories—The Most Heroic Romans—Despite Rome's Majesty—The Riches of Empire—Why the Hero Wept—The Acts of Martyrs—Our Richest Age...................................... 83-96

CHAPTER VIII

THE MIRROR OF CHRIST'S HUMANITY—The Harvest of Reverent Minds—All Living Things—The Tribes of Men — The Peerless Christ — Poetic Greece — Imagined Deities—Fables of Gods and Men—Christ's Great Command—The Fount of Charity—The Mirror of the Father.. 97-109

CHAPTER IX

THE MIRROR OF CHRIST'S YOUTH—Weavers of Myths—The Dreams of Jews—The Winner of Hearts—As a Little Child—For the Lowliest—"Great Little One!"—Immortal Memories—All Ages Sanctified—From Christ's Eyes..... ..110-122

CHAPTER X

THE MIRROR OF CHRIST'S MANHOOD—Knowledge and Love—The Word Made Flesh—To the Lowly and Poor—Compassion on the Multitude—The Miracles of Mercy—The Love of the People—Another Kindly Miracle—A Man Entirely Godlike—Our Blessed Lot—"Come to Me!"......123-135

CHAPTER XI

THE MIRROR OF CHRIST'S PASSION—The Amazing Prayer—The Figure on the Cross—Christ's Sufferings—The Sublimest Mirror of Love—"How He Loves Me!"—The Wooing of Hearts—The Victory of Love—A Prayer for Love—"O Christ, Be Pitiful!"........................136-146

LIST OF ILLUSTRATIONS

Facing
Page

REX REGUM—The King of Kings—by Van Eyck.............. 11

LANDSCAPE—by Jacob Van Ruisdael........................ 31

THE FOREST—by Jacob Van Ruisdael...................... 63

LANDSCAPE—by Jacob Van Ruisdael........................ 87

LANDSCAPE WITH MILL—by Claude de Lorraine.......... 103

CHRIST ON THE CROSS—by Velasquez................... 135

"In Christ, we shall find visible the beauty and lovableness of the Uncreated God."

(Rex Regum—The King of Kings—by Van Eyck)

MIRRORS OF GOD

CHAPTER I

GOD'S LOVABLENESS

UR HEART is made for love. Indeed, love is the life of our heart. From the very first days of our conscious existence, when, as children, we became aware of our own selves and of the world around us, we have attached ourselves to persons, places, and things with instinctive affection. Our faculty of love is like a noble vine, which rises from the earth with the impulse to seek some object about which it can cling. A vine is by nature prone to twine itself around, to embrace and hold to something other than itself. With sensitive tendrils it leans this way and that, seeking a support about which it can cling, and if it gains a firm hold upon some comely tree, it will rise high in the air, put forth leaves and flowers, and so identify itself with its support that storms only bind it firmer and winds and rain but wed it closer to the trunk to which it clings. Does this comparison please you? Let us develop it and bring it home to ourselves.

The Tendrils of the Heart

Our heart is by nature prone to twine, to climb, and to cling. Our affections, in childhood, reach out the tendrils of their preference and twist about the objects we find around us. Love we must; it is one of the greatest needs of our being, and at first our childish love attaches itself almost by instinct to mother and father, to others about us, to places, to toys.

But as our will grows stronger and our intelligence develops, we can choose and determine what we shall love. Free beings, we are not moved only by necessary instincts like the brutes. Intelligence enlightens our will and our lordly will can so far direct its own decisions as to select the objects of its love. How tremendous are the consequences that wait upon that selection! How profoundly are we ourselves made or marred by the things upon which we fix our hearts!

Let us pursue the comparison of the growing vine. Sometimes, finding nothing to which to cling, or perversely refusing other supports, the vine will twine about its own stem, twisting and interweaving its tendrils and branches with each other, matting leaves and stems together, sprawling upon the ground, perplexed and bound in its own entangling embraces, until it becomes an ugly and misshapen thing, a figure of selfish and introspective folly.

GOD'S LOVABLENESS

If we love our own selves, turn our affections back on their source, and refuse them the support their nature craves for, our heart becomes as the tangled vine,—matted and sodden with earthly selfishness!

PRONE ON THE EARTH

That same vine, whose nature it is to rise high in the air and sunshine, may grow rank over the low weeds and bushes at either side. This is ruinous to its health and beauty. The poor, weak vegetation, close to the ground, is no fit support for a vine which nature meant to rise far above the undergrowth of the forest. It devours the rank weeds with its eager tendrils, but they cannot support it, and again the vine becomes a sorry object, sprawling on the earth instead of rising high in the air.

Our heart has a similar fate when it clings to the creatures around it and does not take care to rise and seek its due support and rightful anchorage. Let your affections run along the ground, fix them merely on creatures about you, and, whether you perceive it or not, you become of the earth—earthy, low-looking, unaspiring, altogether caught and snared in the weeds of life and time.

The glory of the vine is when it seizes an upspringing trunk and mounts heavenwards. Then, its leaves spread to the sun and its flowers nod on the breezes. It has found its rightful support, and comes to its kingdom. Of the earth, yet uplifted far above it, slight and unstable of itself, yet borrowing all the height and strength and sureness of the tree to which it clings, the vine rejoices in health and beauty. So, too, does our heart, when our love has found its proper object and learned to mount heavenwards! The instinct of our heart, like the instinct of the vine, is to climb and to cling. If it clings without climbing, if it twines about some object never meant to lift it to light and joy, whether that object is self or the creatures of earth loved for their own sake merely, it grovels on the ground.

THE CRAVING FOR GOD

The love for which our heart was made, the destined support and stay which is to lift it up and let it blossom and grow beautiful, is the love of God, and of ourselves and our neighbor for the sake of God. Until it has seized hold on this love and twined so close about it that it becomes one with it, our heart is never quiet nor satisfied. It keeps reaching out the tendrils of its affection towards one thing after another, never content with what it seizes. The supports of creatures allure it, but do not sustain it. Restlessness and craving, the constant wishing for new objects of delight, incessant changing of desires, these are sure signs of a need never satisfied, an instinct never fulfilled, a natural want that is never sated with the true object of its pursuit. "Our hearts, O God," cried out St. Augustine, "were made for Thee, and they will never rest nor be satisfied until they possess Thee!"

Not until Heaven welcomes us will our hearts possess God in the full and perfect measure that is needed to satisfy their immense desires. But there is a heaven-on-

earth, which consists in loving God most of all and cleav-
ing to Him with so faithful a love that all other loves and
inclinations rest on this, spring from this, and are mod-
erated and controlled according to their due measure and
proportion to the love of God. When this Divine Lover
supports and lifts up the heart of man, that heart forgets
its natural fickleness and weakness; it cleaves to God and
to His will as the vine weds itself to its supporting tree.

WHY IS IT HARD TO LOVE?

I seem to hear someone ask: "But if our hearts were
made for the love of God and if this is their destined
object and highest purpose—to love Him, why is it not
easier to love Him? Why do the loves of creatures enter
into and possess our hearts which were formed for God?"
Ah! that is indeed a mystery, to fathom which one must
sound the depths of our human weakness and misery. It
is most true that our hearts were created for the love of
God. But the ignorance of our intellect, the greed of our
senses, the perversity of our will, wounded by sin, turn us
away from our true object and send our heart wandering
after things that cannot satisfy its hunger. Did we see
God as the just in heaven see Him, were we face to face
with His infinite perfection, could we realize that He is
the uncreated Source of all beauty, goodness, power,
wisdom, holiness, and is Himself the self-existing and
infinite Ideal, the Good for Whom our blind hearts yearn
forever—then indeed we could not choose but love Him.

But such a vision and such a revelation are for heaven,

not for earth, for the state of perfect fruition not for this
time of trial and probation. Here on earth we are put to
the test to see whether we will love God freely and obey
Him faithfully, knowing Him dimly as in a glass by the
light of reason and faith. Did we see God as He is we
could not choose but love Him, but our love would be
unmeritorious because it would not be free. That we may
merit, God gives us light indeed enough to discern His
perfections, but not the blazing light of Glory which would
compel us to love and to serve.

The Ways of Knowledge

The way then to the more perfect love of God is
through the more perfect knowledge of His divine excellences. That infinite Beauty, Strength, and Truth need but
to be known to be loved. Yet, alas! our knowledge of God
must come from our own laborious strivings to know Him
more perfectly. Since we may not now see Him as He is,
we must learn of Him from the dim but sufficient mirror
of His creatures, reading the great book of His creation
which declares Him, seeking Him in human nature which
He has so wonderfully made to His image and likeness,
listening to the voice of Faith which teaches of Him;
piecing together, so to say, with unwearying care, all the
hints and lineaments of His own perfection which He, the
Maker and Model of all things, has mercifully left upon
all His various handiwork.

Now we think, perhaps, that it is strange how God
conceals Himself in His own universe. He is everywhere,

the one all-pervading and self-existing Reality, from Whom all things else spring as from their first cause; and yet, He is unseen and unheard in the midst of the bewildering beauty and variety of His own creation. His name is written neither upon the earth nor upon the sky, His accents never sound in the ears of His creatures. Though He is endlessly near to all things, and supports with such constant care the slightest object He has made, for without his unceasing power it would sink back into its original nothingness, still there is no immediate sign to make us conscious of His presence. The All-Beautiful is hidden from us, the All-Good is mysterious to us, the All-True and All-Holy is beyond our ken.

For Our Merit

It is for our merit that God would have it so. He could manifest Himself to us in more moving ways, if He would. He could descend and walk with us in a visible form as He walked with Adam in the morning airs. He might, if He wished, almost compel our love. He prefers to leave us free. All about us, if we will only see them, are hints and traces of His loveliness. Within us, the still, small voice of our conscience reminds us constantly of the law of God. The splendid order of all creation proclaims its uncreated cause. God's wisdom is manifested in the harmony of things, His beauty in the loveliness of His creation, His power in its magnificence, His generosity in its vastness and splendor, His goodness in the admirable supplying of all our needs.

[17]

Our own body and soul with their wonderful gifts—the natures of other men, the myriad richness of the sky and earth and sea, the countless stars of night, the freshness and beauty of dawn and sunset, the procession of the seasons, the history of nations, the variety of countries and of cities, the treasures of art, the discoveries of science—all that is and that we can perceive or know is but a mirror in which to look and learn of the goodness, power, wisdom, and all the other attributes of that eternal Creator and Lord of all Whom we call God.

It is only our own dullness, which we must overcome by study, thought, and prayer, that keeps us from knowing, admiring, and loving with an immense and devoted love, this Being Whose munificence and glory shine so clearly from the face of all things. In itself, creation is admirably adapted to teach us and to lead us to the footstool of the Most High. But we must labor and struggle to learn this easy lesson, as a poor simpleton puzzles and frets to understand a plain task, not because the matter is hard but because his wits are dull. Sin has set our faculties awry and made it easy for us to turn aside to things of sense and hard to seek the things that are of God. Besides, being creatures of clay, dependent on our senses for the beginnings of all our knowledge, it is difficult for us to rise to things unseen. Our fleshly eyes are not proportioned to the vision of God. We must behold Him now as it were in a glass, darkly, by the contemplation of His attributes as they are manifested in His creation.

Only in heaven shall we see Him face to face and know Him as we are known.

THE NEED OF EFFORT

All the more reason for setting ourselves diligently to work to know and to love God. Any effort would be worth while when there is question of achieving the one end for which we are made, of reaching the highest and noblest purpose of our being. If it is difficult for us to know and love God as we should, the very difficulty should spur us on to more energetic striving. If we love God as we ought, all other goods will come to us together with that love. But, unless we love Him as we should, no other good can bring us contentment, for He alone is able to fill and satisfy the infinite craving of our heart.

We, who have the true faith, are of all men best able to know God and to love Him. Even the pagans, as St. Paul tells us, can learn His unseen goodness and beauty from the things that are seen of His creation. But for the unaided human intelligence, distracted and led away by earthly speculations and darkened by sin, the task is a difficult one. The greatest of pagan philosophers had but a dim and imperfect knowledge of God compared to the glorious and admirable teaching concerning Him which our faith affords us. We are given, from God Himself, a lovely and inspiring sum of teaching concerning His nature, His attributes, and His works most suited to move us to an adoring and devoted love.

[19]

MIRRORS OF GOD

The Book of Love

What our faith teaches us concerning God, His goodness, His power, and His love, the visible universe illustrates and confirms. The world, with its variety and splendor, its wonder and charm, its endless manifestations of wisdom of plan and power of execution, is like an outspread book in which we are to read of the lovableness of God. When we look with understanding and reverent eyes on His handiwork, and remember that there is no spark of beauty or gleam of wonder in the whole world but comes from Him, then we can better comprehend in our dim way how worthy He is to be loved, and how fit and necessary it is for us to love Him with our whole heart, our whole mind, our whole soul, and all our strength as He wishes and commands us.

Thus, learning about God and realizing the lovableness of God, our heart will find its destined support and stay, and will twine its restless tendrils upon that one trunk of safety and assurance that can lift it up from the earth and bear it towards the heavens. Then indeed will that unquiet heart have peace, for there is only one God that can satisfy its unbounded hunger, one Faith that can assuage its ceaseless thirst for beauty and delight. "Our heart, O God, was made for Thee and to enjoy Thee. How then, can it rest until it rests in Thee?"

CHAPTER II

THE MIRROR OF MEN

*T*HE SUN beams in the summer heavens, and his flooding rays light up a whole hemisphere of earth. The continents bask in his radiance, the watery plains of ocean cast back his beauty from the facets of their millions of waves, the streams run bright with his silver, the cup of every flower shines with delicate color which it has borrowed from the magical and prismatic glory prisoned in every one of his clear white rays. When he shines forth in all his splendor, the whole world glows with various beauty. The huge undulations of the forests are clothed with shimmering green, the beds of blossoms shine with beauty, the sea is amethystine in its depths and emerald in its shallows, the sky is like a dome of azure crystal, luminous as a jewel.

All this various color, luster, and glow of nature are borrowed from the sun. All else is beautiful only in so far as it mirrors his single and self-sufficient radiance. Science assures us that the white ray of the sun has in it the vibrations of all the colors of the spectrum, and when its beam falls on any earthly thing, it breaks into its component colors, some of which are absorbed and never reach our eyes; others are flung back and speeding through the ether produce on our optic nerve the sensation which we call the sight of color. Thus the blending of the primal colors, of violet, indigo, blue, green, yellow, orange, and red make up the color of the world and all things are but imperfect mirrors of the sun's unique and limpid radiance.

WHEN LIGHT DEPARTS

We may realize this when twilight falls, when the day yields to night. Then all things lose their bright colors. Their shapes loom indistinctly through the darkness. The tints which made the sky beautiful and the sea glorious have gone with the sun. It was the sun that gave the green to the grass and trees, the red to the roses, the white to the lilies, and the hues of rubies and sapphires to the little flowers of the field. We cannot bear to gaze at the sun; its radiance is too keen and strong for our fleshly eyes to endure, but we can perceive its beauty in the mirrors of the earth.

There is no need to develop the application of this metaphor to our knowledge and our love of God. He is the uncreated Sun of the universe, Whose power and beauty illumine all creatures, giving them whatever loveliness and lovableness they possess. The light of the earthly sun is so intense and pours forth in such copious streams, that for our small vision it is overpowering, and it offers a comparison for the eternal beauty. But God is in sober truth infinitely beautiful and lovable. In Him are all blessed traits of amiability and perfection, and in a manner without bounds or limits. Whatever we see in His creatures, we may use to help us to conjecture His lovableness, without fear of forming an ideal too glorious or too great. For God is infinitely lovable, and therefore, whatever we think of Him that is good and glorious falls short of the sublime reality by as much as our limited minds fall short of the infinite.

THE MIRRORS OF CREATION

Still, we may forever increase in the knowledge and love of God by contemplating Him in His mirrors of creation. Each creature has something to reveal to us of the divine perfections. In the beginning, when throughout eternity God existed alone, because it is His nature to exist and He sustains Himself by His own power of being, God contemplated His own essence and saw therein all the possibilities of imitating it in creatures. He is the exemplar and the model of all created loveliness; He is Himself the source of all the vast design of the universe. Hence, every creature has in it some resemblance to God and can in so far declare the nature and attributes of its Maker.

The insensate world, the huge masses and forms of inanimate matter, the bulk of the continents, the depths of the ocean, the interminable harmony of the stars, the great bulks of summer clouds, the far prospects of wintry wastes of snow, the peace of limitless seas, the pour of mighty rivers, the resistless sweep of winds, the flaming of lightning, the roar of tempests, all these signs and manifestations of the boundless powers of nature mirror in a faint way the might and grandeur of God. They witness to His creative power and they do more; they give a faint notion of His limitless energy, of His immeasurable strength to rule and to sustain all this creation. The vastness, the weight, and the momentum of the heavenly bodies, which surpass our extremest imaginings, the awful elemental power of natural forces, the torrential force of water, the fearful destructiveness of air when it rages in tornado or hurricane, and the sudden bright terror of lightning are dreadful to our weakness. They are as nothing to the power of God. He holds the universe easily in leash. The most stupendous of natural forces obey His commands like the weakest. He could intolerably multiply all the awful energy of earth and sky until they made our helpless bodies and souls cower in fear, and could still control them as easily and as utterly as He does the present order of nature. Whirlwinds and thunder, ice and snow, the rush of waters, the fury of winds, all proclaim, as the Psalmist again and again reminds us, the endlessly greater and more majestic power of God.

CLEARER AND CLEARER

As we rise in the scale of creation, we see the attributes of God more and more clearly mirrored in creatures. Even the smallest living thing is a greater wonder in its way than all the harmony of the heavens. Indeed, the development of the microscope and the painstaking investigations of living processes which it has made possible, disclose to us a universe of singular order and harmony in the smallest living organism. Living beings are either made up of tiny cells, or are composed, in the case of the lowest forms of life, of a single cell, which exists and propagates its kind in a microscopic world of its own. The wisdom and the love wherewith God has designed and preserves His creatures shine forth in these fragile beings, infinitesimally small, yet capable of maintaining their little spark of life against the warfare of their environment.

The more perfect and beautiful the organization of living creatures, the more they show forth the love and skill of their Creator, and the more they imitate His unique and uncreated perfection. Thus, a great tree of the forest, which spreads its huge limbs overhead and sinks its gnarled roots into the ground, which breathes the air through its thousands of leaves and wrestles with the wind of tempestuous nights or sleeps under sunny noons of summer, speaks to us without words of the goodness of God. Remember the forest, with its murmurous silences, the dappling of sunshine through innumerable leaves, the green life of old trees, and think how they proclaim the goodness and the wisdom of God. So do the frail flowers which blossom about the tree trunks, so do the vines which clamber around them, with the grass of meadows and the tangle of summer thickets, sweet with flowers, all speak eloquently of God.

The Sentient World

But when we ascend yet another step and come to the animal world, we see still plainer indications of God's presence and power. The senses of animals, their powers of motion, the keen unerring instincts which guide them, the beauty of their forms, the splendor of their hues, the swiftness and power of their motions, all proclaim the glory of their Creator. For God found in Himself the ideas of all these marvelous creatures. He looked at His own essence, than which nothing else existed from the beginning, and beheld that it could be imitated in these various forms of being. They all, therefore, express in some sort His divine perfections. They all mirror back something of His life, His strength, and His beauty, as the various forms and colors of earth flash back in some way the white radiance of the glorious sun.

Think of the wonder and variousness of the animal world! How it swarms on earth, from the fauna of tropical countries, the leopards which stalk through the jungles of Asia, the lions that roar in the desert, the bright colored birds that chatter and fly through the heavy creepers of the sultry forests of Africa, to the lithe and swift wild things of the poles, white as their native snows and running silently along the never-melting ice cliffs. Think of the charming fauna of our own temperate climes, the animals which are the friends of mankind; the horse with his speed and strength, his amazing instinct, his fidelity to his master; the dog with his constant companionship with man. These creatures of God manifest, each in its own way, the perfection of the power which brought them into being. These animals, the highest of the brutes, can become so truly the friends of their owners that when they die men weep as though bereaved of a dear, human intimate.

MIRROR OF MEN

The Sea Gulls

We think it wonderful, and rightly so, that at last, after many ages, human intelligence and ingenuity have succeeded in devising machines heavier than air which will actually fly through that impalpable element. But consider the seagulls, how they soar in the teeth of the blast. Who that has watched them from the stern of a great sea-going vessel was not amazed at their uncanny powers of flight. While the great ship is straining all its engines to breast the fierce wind, these birds match the speed of the boat with scarcely an effort of their wings. They swoop and soar in great circles, following the ship. No labor of the flapping wings is theirs, yet they are borne along at a dizzy speed. Watch them closely and you shall see the astounding ease with which they keep their perfect balance against the thrust and pull of the vortices of the air. It is God Who makes these marvelous creatures, not, according to the ways of man, in a noisy workshop with painful measurement and precise toil, but as easily as the tiny cell grows to the adult bird, by imperceptible changes, first a chick, then a fledgling, then a young gull, taught by subtle instinct to winnow the air with its wings, and slant, and sail secure on the rude gales above the tossing sea. How even the least of these wild, graceful creatures proclaims the wonder and power of its Maker, more than any books written by learned sages or poems of imperishable skill!

MIRRORS OF GOD

Creation's Chasm

But when we pass from even the most splendid of the brute creation to the least of the tribes of men, we overstep a huge chasm in creation. For man, though he has in common with the insensate world a body which is material, though he shares life with the plants, and sense, motion, instinct and the power of locomotion with brute animals, is, besides, a being of intelligence and free will. Even the simplest savage is immeasurably above the noblest of the brutes, because he can understand and reason. He can, moreover, exercise the power of free choice and can determine deliberately whether he will do this or that, will follow one or the other of two courses, will yield to persuasion or resist it. The brutes have no such power, either of understanding or of choice. Their instinct and their animal powers are, indeed, so wonderful as sometimes to simulate intelligence and free will. But in point of fact, as scientists like Fabre have demonstrated, they never really reason nor will. Everything they do is the result of instinct and natural impulse. They have no control over their destiny, but do as nature bids them, with inevitable and blind obedience.

Read Fabre, the Homer of the insects, whose marvelous observations have opened to man a new universe of insect life. He describes, with absorbing interest, his shrewd experiments with ants, with wasps, with bees, with scorpions, creatures in whom natural instinct is developed to a degree so extraordinary as to make one almost tempted to suspect their historian of exaggeration. But Fabre shows by his ingenious experiments that when these insects seem to show the most intelligence in their actions, they are most apt to be led by the blind following of their instinct into egregious blunders. When the environment is altered so as to set a trap for them, where intelligence could leap over, instinct falls into the snare.

THE INTELLIGENCE OF MAN

Man, therefore, is alone in all the material creation possessed of an intelligence and of the constant companion of intelligence—free will. It is he only who can look about on the works of God and admire them. He alone most perfectly represents the intelligence and free will of his Creator. We may gain great knowledge of God and God's lovableness from contemplating the rest of His creation. Earth and sky and sea, with their multitudinous wonders, can tell us much of Him Who made them. From the oozy bed of the deepest ocean, where strange sea creatures creep and swim under the pressure of intolerable tons of salt water, to the summits of cloud-piercing mountains, where the thin air barely supports the laboring wings of birds, every creature eloquently proclaims the beauty and amiability of Him Who planned and made it of His own free and intelligent power. But more than all other beings, man is the image and likeness of God, because man bears, in his intellect and will, a resemblance to his Creator, unspeakably more close than the brute creation can show.

God is a pure spirit; that is to say, He is free from all

conditions of space, matter, and time. The manner of God's existence we cannot imagine, because all our perceptions are of material things. Our eyes can only measure and perceive the vibration of the ether, which we call light, and which produces in them the impressions of form and color. God makes no such impressions, because His being is too fine and perfect thus to affect our eyes. He is everywhere but imperceptible by us, not on account of any imperfection of His own but because of our limitations. Hence, all material things resemble God only distantly. They have being as He has being; they have goodness borrowed from Him as He has uncreated goodness; they have truth because they are imitations in some sort of His unlimited truth; but their resemblance to Him is a very imperfect one.

GOD'S IMAGE IN OUR SPIRIT

Every man, besides his body, has a spiritual soul. He is, therefore, a spirit as well as a material being. His body is the image of God, so far as it expresses what God saw in His own substance, when He decided to create the body of man; His soul is much more like God because it, also, is a spirit, having intelligence and free will, and of another order of being from mere matter. This soul of man most nearly resembles God. By thinking of what we know of man, especially of his intellectual and volitional life, we can learn a great deal about the dignity, goodness, beauty, and lovableness of man's Maker.

Recall to mind the many things you know about the intellectual and spiritual life of the noblest men and

"The sun beams, and his flooding rays light up a whole hemisphere of earth!"

(Landscape by Jacob Van Ruisdael)

women. In its highest reaches, our human nature is surely wonderful and sublime. Our senses, sight, hearing, taste and touch, and smell are the only gateways through which knowledge of the outside world can come to us, and everything we know is gained through these senses or through the conclusions which our intelligence draws from what we see, hear, taste, feel, or smell.

Yet, in spite of all the handicaps to our knowledge, how amazing are the triumphs of the intelligence of man. Through the slow progress of generations, men have searched out the obscure and difficult secrets of science. They have devised cunning lenses and made microscopes and telescopes; the one to explore the unfathomable abysses of the heavens; the other to reveal that infinitesimal universe which trembles in every water drop and lurks in the tiniest particle of living substance. Science is wonderful, but we should never forget that it is all the achievement of one of God's creatures. If the knowledge of man is marvelous, how great is the Creator Who made man to His own image and likeness, and gave him intelligence which could search out such new worlds of knowledge!

THE CREATIVE IMAGINATION

Again, consider the creative imagination of mankind. Helped by that same human intelligence, what astounding achievements it has reached in every department of art! The traveller in the old countries of Europe is forever astonished at the richness of the priceless heritage of architecture, painting, and sculpture, which is the possession of great cities and nations, of churches and museums in those lands where the great masters flourished, or whither their works came by purchase or by gift.

The cathedrals of the middle ages, volumes, or rather, whole libraries in stone, which still lift their memorable fronts against the storms and suns of these latest times, are an epitome of human intelligence and imagination. Richly crusted as they are with symbolic sculptures, crowded with historic images, adorned with masterpieces of painting and carving, they form the sublimest monuments to human genius. In the full museums, also, the walls gleam with priceless pictures, the work of men whose minds and hands praised God with color, and light, and shade, as the poet does with glowing syllables, or the musician with sublime and harmonious sounds. Gazing on these supreme triumphs of creative art, we cannot help admiring the native powers and the painstaking and laborious skill and art of the men who wrought them. But these men, in turn, were the masterpieces of God and their intelligence and creative power were but a faint copy of the uncreated original of all goodness, beauty, and truth.

MAN'S GODLIKE WILL

If the power of man's mind can astonish us and raise us to heights where we can contemplate the uncreated intelligence of God, the power of His will is equally wonderful. In fact, the moral grandeur of mankind is even more impressive and brings us nearer to an understanding of God's lovableness than the power of his intelligence.

The one lordliest faculty of man, his most Godlike possession, is the power of his free will, by which he can rule his own destiny, deliberately choose what is good and noble, persist in a definite course of action, even against the most desperate odds, and exhibit sublime moral courage and power in spite of his puny physical strength.

Call to mind the great exemplars of moral courage, the men and women of whom history tells us, who almost justify that sublime boast of the poet Horace, when he declared that a just man and one who was steadfast in his will would bear unflinchingly the crashing fragments of the world, though the whole universe were to topple down in ruins. At its best, the human will, even left to its natural powers, can achieve sublime heroism. The Roman heroes of the days of the republic were men in whom courage subdued the natural shrinkings of our flesh to a degree altogether wonderful and amazing. But when the grace of God is added to the natural vigor of the human will, the heroism of man surpasses any praise.

JEWISH AND CHRISTIAN HEROES

Remember the heroic figures of the Old Testament; the Prophets, like Isaias and Elias, who defied the despotic power of kings; the judges, like Samuel, who withstood the will of the people, for the sake of the will of God; the Maccabees, with their preterhuman courage, devoting themselves to death for the sake of their nation and their law. These men were Godlike in the power of their will. They lift us up through the contemplation of their heroism, to

[33]

that uncreated Goodness and Strength Whose will is irresistible and all-powerful, Whose single command brought the universe into being and struck order out of chaos by one almighty "fiat."

But the Christian heroes display a yet greater sublimity of moral grandeur. Consider the innumerable host of martyrs, who laid down their lives, ground by the teeth of beasts or stricken with unspeakable and barbarous tortures, for the sake of truth. Remember the long line of confessors who suffered slow and unbloody martyrdoms for faith and principle. The mere mention of these Christian heroes elevates the heart and stirs the intelligence to the contemplation of Him from Whom they took their being. If man, in his intelligence and free will, is so noble and lovable, how amiable is God, the Source of his being and excellence. In the mirror of noble men, we may contemplate the beauty and lovableness of God.

CHAPTER III

THE MIRROR OF THE STARS

IT IS our unfortunate limitation to be obliged to get all our immediate knowledge of others from our five senses. What we can hear, can see, can touch, or taste, or smell, we know quite definitely and from experience. It is this direct knowledge which most impresses us and allures us. Most persons find it hard to realize and to love things which they cannot hear, see, or experience directly. This is one of the reasons why they find it hard to love God as they should.

God is all beautiful; His perfect substance contains in itself eminently and to a supreme degree, all true beauty. Any lovely person or thing which we can see or know directly is a very faint hint, a most imperfect suggestion of the loveliness of God. Reason compels us to admit this, for God has created all things and He must possess completely and to a sublime degree what He gives to His creation. The sun must have in itself more light and heat than the rays it sends into our eyes; the stream or the spring must possess a greater wealth of waters than the rill that it gives to slake our thirst.

Besides, since the eternal and infinite Creator is endlessly superior in every way to His creation, He must possess to an unimaginable degree all the charms and beauties which He has given to them. God is moreover infinite, and this means that His beauty and His charm, like all other perfections in His being, are without bounds. He is lovable beyond all measure, and we should love Him without measure. But to do this, we have to make efforts to bring home to ourselves the lovableness of God. It is not enough for us that He is in Himself all lovable. We ourselves must realize this, must grasp it not only in theory but with a vividness of apprehension which will move our heart to true and mighty love.

"Lift Up Your Hearts!"

The beauty of nature is capable of raising our hearts to God and helping us to love Him. Indeed, it is for this that nature was made, to declare to man the lovableness of its Creator. Unfortunately, many ardent lovers of nature stop short with the creature and never care to go farther than the surface of the world's loveliness. They are like men who love books for the beauty of their binding and never wish to read the contents, or like visitors to rare museums of the works of the masters who look with pleasure on the bright tints, the harmonious forms of their paintings and never seek to know the deep significance of their art, much less to learn the painter's name and history.

What would a poet, who had used all the resources of his art to express the most noble enthusiasms and loyalties of his soul, and had with loving care written his poems in fair characters on snowy parchment, think of that fantastic reader who paid no heed to the sense of the bright words, but only dwelt on the clear hue of the page, the rounded beauty of the writing? Or, how would the painter who had spent laborious and painful days in making his canvas glow with thought and vision, judge the man who looked in rapture at the tints upon his canvas and neither cared what the artist had sought to express, nor who he was who had so wrought these pure harmonies of color and forms of loveliness?

Neglect—Uncouth and Barbarous

To admire nature without loving God is a far more uncouth and barbarous procedure. For the poet and the painter only combine and adapt the beauties which they find in creation. They are not the exemplars and originals of the great works which their genius executes. But in nature, God has first conceived the plan and then spread it forth in reality. He is at the same time the original well-spring of all created loveliness, the poet and artist Who has brought it to be, and the Framer of the vast canvas of the universe on which these beauties are spread forth. The heavens and earth bear witness to His glory and His lovableness. The heavens declare the glory of God, and His unbounded worthiness to be loved. But it is the misfortune of our small and limited intelligence to find it so hard to grasp the message, written in flaming characters across the face of the firmament.

Recall to yourself some clear and beautiful night of summer. Wherever you dwell, whether in city or country, in temperate, or frigid, or torrid climes, you must be familiar with God's splendid and unfathomable skies. You have seen their deep loveliness, flaming over the tall roofs of huddled cities, or mirrored in the smooth bosoms of placid lakes, or beaming in tranquil splendor over broad stretches of pleasant countryside, or twinkling with their points of vivid flame above the breast of the ocean, smooth in placid calm or tossing back the starbeams from the curling crests of its wind-driven waves. Everyone who has eyes to see has beheld this greatest and most far-flung of all creation's spectacles. Our eyes are too weak to pierce earthly distances; a few score of miles is the extreme range of their vision. But from any poor vantage-point of earth, looking upward at the stars, we can see to distances which border on infinity. The steady ray which enters our eyes from some of these unwinking starry presences may have left the sun from which it streams twenty thousand years ago and voyaged down the ethereal pathways of the sky, traveling nearly two hundred thousand miles for every second of that immense duration, until it prints its message of pure light upon the retina of our eye.

THE SKY'S VAST ABYSSES

The figures in which we are accustomed to compute earthly distances fail so utterly to describe these vast abysses of the heavens, that astronomers have been fain to invent a new unit to measure the distances of the stars. This unit is the light-year, or the space over which a ray of light would travel in an entire year. The measured speed of light is some hundred and eighty thousand miles a second. Every minute, therefore, the light from a star travels some ten million eight hundred thousand miles; in a single hour this ray of light voyages six hundred and forty-eight million miles; in a day, keeping its incredible speed, it will have traveled fifteen billion, five hundred and fifty-five million miles. Conceive then, if you can, what a vast distance it has covered in its flight during the twenty thousand years it has been seeking your humble eye, to bear to you its luminous message of the greatness and lovableness of its Creator!

Have you ever lain prostrate on the warm, summer earth and let your eyes explore at leisure the ethereal distances? You seemed floating in space; the trivial details of earth's bounded landscape disappeared from your ken. You were like a disembodied soul, upheld in the clear heavens to contemplate their unearthly loveliness. From verge to verge of the sky, you saw the white glimmer of the milky way, that astounding ribbon of light whereof the warp and woof are stars, constellations, nebulae. The feebleness of our sight cannot distinguish its component luminaries. Seen through the telescope, it breaks up into hundreds of thousands of stars and clusters of stars, of vast nebular masses, whirling in the fiery throes of the birth of worlds and suns, of systems greater by far than our sun and its planets, of galaxies of light which the creative hand of God has strewn like sand across the shores of His vast oceans of the heavens.

MIRRORS OF GOD

THE UNCHANGING STARRY SCENERY

Your eyes sought out the familiar landmarks of the stellar scenery. There were the Great Bear, and the Lesser Bear, performing their solemn dance about the polar star, as the shepherds of Chaldea saw them cycles ago, as Adam and Eve beheld them first from the calm alleys of Paradise, as Noah watched them from his ship in the streaming waters, as Abraham looked upon them from the plains of Mambre, and as David saw them and sang on his harp of the splendors of the skies. There is Orion, with his gleaming belt and sword, a great cross in the sky, whereat perhaps the Blessed Mary looked in prophecy when she sat with her Son and St. Joseph at their cottage door in Nazareth, after the day's work was done, and gazed in prayerful silence at the bright stars which He had made while He was in the bosom of His Father.

You greeted the dear and familiar constellations, sloping up from the under horizon or leaning down the long pathway towards the West, and you exulted in their beauty, as every generation has exulted from the days of Father Adam, as everyone shall exult until the spasm of judgment shakes the sky and tumbles the stars from their high firmament. For even the stupendous handwriting of God upon the heavens is but a passing message of His love and power. Vast as are these illimitable bulks of suns and stars that fly so smoothly down the invisible grooves of the sky, they are like grains of sand to Him Who has weighed them in the palm of His hand, has poised them in their appointed orbits, and sustains their mighty and ponderous being as easily as He does the almost invisible motes that whirl in every sunbeam.

But did your heart, as you surveyed the stars, leap with pure love for the august and amiable Creator of this wide-flung splendor? Did you rise in thought beyond the pales of creation, sending your soul to knock at the pearly gates of inaccessible light where dwells the infinitely lovely and lovable Source of all this light and beauty? It is for this that the stars were made. They are heralds, messengers, ambassadors to our hearts through our eyes. So much does God desire the love of man, that all the mazy orbits of the sky, all the incredible weight of suns and worlds, and all the ethereal harmony of nebulae and planets are but a slight price for Him to pay for our love.

THE UNIVERSE OF STARS

Look forth, in vivid fancy, into the universe of stars. Compel your sluggish imagination to conceive those myriad orbs, those fathomless distances. Soar forth in spirit and visit the distant planets. See the splendor of the rings of Saturn, spreading their vast disks of light athwart the blue sky like emblems of eternity. Hear the titanic roarings of the flames of Jupiter, that burning star whose ardours shake the ether. These are the small satellites of our little sun which is one of the lesser among heaven's luminaries. Then go further, swing out upon the mightier suns, so vast and great that our whole planetary system is like a grain of sand in comparison with their huge orbs of flame.

Behold the splendors of this celestial scenery, where the eyes of your flesh would wither and shrivel up with too much glory. Your eyes indeed can discern mercifully only the distant glimmer of these fields of light, of these oceans of fire. The mountainous emanations of keen flame leap up from the surface of the orbs for hundreds of thousands of miles, the cracklings of their vast explosions detonating with stupendous force and energy. Even when we look at our own small moon through the telescope, the grandeur of its pale scenery fills us with awe. What must be the immense effulgence of living suns, the luminous beauty of vast nebulae, the huge and splendid arcs of solar scenery where the mountains are bulks of flaming light and the oceans are pits of molten stone. How these sublime suggestions of astronomy proclaim the glory of God!

Thus, the discoveries of science join with the imaginations of poets and of saints to help us realize and love the goodness and power of God from the glory of His star-strewn heavens. Dante loved the stars, and each of the great divisions of his stupendous trilogy, the Inferno, the Purgatorio, and the Paradiso, ends with the mention of these celestial witnesses, "thence issuing we again beheld the stars." St. Ignatius loved to contemplate that heavenly spectacle from the balcony of his humble room, and he was wont to say, "How vile earth seems when I look upwards at the heavens." The Little Flower of Jesus, Soeur Therese of Lisieux, tells us with what rapturous joy she sat with her sister at the great window of their attic play-room and read the true teaching of the stars concerning the greatness of God, the splendor of His beauty, and the nothingness of this earth in comparison with His eternal recompenses.

A Cry of Love

Let us also, therefore, learn to read in this immortal splendor of the heavens, this unchanging witness of the love, and power and beauty of the Creator. Let us, in the presence of the starry night, lift up our hearts to heaven and cry out, "Oh Beauty, ever ancient and ever new, how late and how little have I loved You. Lord God, Creator of the skies, Whose almighty Hand has linked the ponderous orbs of heaven each to each and keeps them in their appointed orbits, sustaining their awful weight and ruling their dizzy swiftness, I love You with all the devotion of my being. I desire to make my love vaster than the suns that swarm by millions, seen and unseen, in the hollow of the sky. I love You for Your own sake, because You are so good in Yourself, and so worthy of all my love. Sublime as is all this starry pageantry, it is but as the fringe on Your garments, the golden dust on the hem of Your robe, the dim glimmering in a darkened mirror of the uncreated and unimagined glory of Your lovableness.

"As the splendor of the sun is mirrored in a drop of water on the grass, so is Your greatness faintly shadowed forth by all this unmeasured grandeur of the heavens. The hollow spaces of the sky, so vast that a beam of light, swiftest of all created things, must labor for thousands of years to span their huge abysses, are naught before the immensity of Your essence, which spans all time and space, actual or to be conceived.

"FOR YOUR OWN SAKE"

"I love You, O my God, Creator of the starry silences, for every one of those swift, impalpable vibrations which speeds into the outer universe from each of these innumerable constellations of golden light. I love You, Planner and Architect of the stars, for every grain of these ponderous suns which swing in glory through the unthinkable abysses of the sky. I love You, Balancer of the stars, Keeper of the golden galaxies, for every hair's breadth of the far-flung orbits of the suns, for every slightest veering of the interwoven paths and courses of these orbed galleons of the sky.

"I love You for Yourself, because You are so good and so worthy of all my love. These splendid and limitless glories of Your creation, the crowded and star-sown fields of the gorgeous and visible heavens are but a tremendous book in which I read suggestions of Your uncreated beauty and lovableness. On the wings of light my soul can soar above creation and find her goal in You. But I love You not alone for Your gifts, but most of all for Yourself. Father, Son, and Holy Ghost, Beauty ever ancient and ever new, Lord of the thronging heavens Whose power and majesty are written in characters of flaming glory across the face of every midnight sky, I love You as David loved You when looking at the stars he sang his psalms of praise, I love You as Mary loved You when she looked upward at the scintillating skies from her cottage door at Nazareth, I love You as Jesus loved You, when, in His long vigils of prayer He turned His eyes, weary with looking at earth, up to the calm, changeless, unfallen beauty of the stars."

CHAPTER IV

THE MIRROR OF HISTORY

*T*HE EARTH is very old. It has been ages on ages since the cloud of vaporous flame which, according to one scientific theory, was to be this planet, cooled and hardened, little by little, into the round globe of seas and continents which we now inhabit. It was ages more, according to the teaching of geology, before the boiling oceans became fit inhabitations for living things, and the harsh outlines of barren and flame-kissed rocks crumbled into soil where plants could cling and flourish. Ages more, and man was created in the person of our first parents, to dwell on this earth and possess it, after the long series of living things, of which the fossil rocks give evidence, had come and gone through the streaming, tropical forests and the swamps, teeming with strange and monstrous life.

DOWN THE CORRIDORS OF HISTORY

How many centuries have elapsed since man was created, and down how many vistas of history his feet have strayed since our father Adam looked up into the sunny skies and about him at the world of living things, and gave each its name according to its kind? The Holy Scriptures, God's inviolable truth, are not intended to serve as a book of the science of natural things nor as a complete treatise on

[46]

human history. Thus, we are left to speculate concerning the age of the world and to piece together from many curious sources the history of man's wanderings over the surface of the earth. The seven "days" of Genesis may be, according to the sense of the Hebrew word, seven aeons of vast duration. The life of man on earth may have already extended into many decades of thousands of years.

But the history of the earth and the history of man, studied from whatever angle and viewed in whatever perfection of detail, are mirrors of the power and goodness, the kindness and lovableness of God, which will help us mightily to know Him and love Him more and more, if only we consider them rightly. We miss the deepest significance of scientific discoveries concerning both these varied and interesting stories of man and his dwelling place, if we fail to refer them to God and to make them the means of loving Him more and more.

New Reasons to Love God

God wishes that mankind should increase forever in knowledge and in goodness, that his increasing discoveries about the past and present of the world he lives in, and about the story of his kind, should more and more reveal to him the goodness of his Maker and the lovableness of a God, Who has wrought so marvelously for mankind. Every new finding of science enriches us with so much more material for knowing God, gives us just so much more reason for loving Him. We, therefore, who are the heirs of all the ages, who are able to utilize all past discoveries and all present researches of geology and history, of the science of the knowledge of the world's adventures as it is spun down the grooves of centuries, and of man's achievements, changes and vicissitudes on earth, are of all generations the richest in the knowledge of God's goodness to mankind.

Besides, every succeeding year piles up a higher monument to God's goodness and amiableness, as the swarming millions of mankind multiply and spread over the surface of the world. The population of the globe is constantly increasing; the achievements of human genius, at least in material invention and development, are constantly growing greater. Every new page of history records more and yet more of the wonders of man and, therefore, gives more and more praise to God Who has created every soul and Who keeps in being, and feeds and watches over every one whom He has made.

THE PAGEANT OF HISTORY

Let us stir within ourselves the magic power of imagination, and see, as though in an inward vision, the course of God's providence throughout human history. The realization of His vast designs, His minute care, and almighty and patient carrying out of His loving provision for men, will surely help us to love Him. Some labor of our mind and imagination is necessary to conceive even faintly of those long, momentous ages, when God worked for us in the solitary moulding of many centuries. Even the comparatively brief history of man on earth bewilders us with its thousands on thousands of eventful years. But it is well worth while to pierce with the laboring wing of fancy the misty reaches of the past, so as to see and to realize how good, how lovable, how endlessly to be thanked and loved is He Whom we call in reverence our God, Creator of the heavens and the earth.

"In the beginning," says the Book of Genesis, "God created heaven and earth, and the earth was void and empty, and darkness was upon the face of the deep." These sublime words, inspired by God, give the first authentic description of one of the earliest scenes in the history of the world. The long ages during which the earth was being prepared for human habitation were over. Out of the welter of molten and gaseous matter, the solid part of the world has cooled into firmness. The boiling oceans had hissed from their confining shores, the vast clouds of vapor had precipitated, and the great outlines of the round and substantial world were revealed for the first time to the light of the sun and the moon, which God had likewise made ready, through the slow shaping of natural powers, to give light and to rule the day and the night.

THE TOIL OF AEONS

During all the aeons which had elapsed from the creation of the material universe until that time, God had been working, according to our manner of speech, to prepare the earth for our indwelling. It was He Who first called the stars and the nebulae into being, and made out of nothing all the material world. Through slow ages, He

[49]

shaped these rude elements, and kept up the weariless power of the forces of nature, until the design of His wisdom began to be realized in the constitution of the earth. How much to be loved is this all-great and all-beautiful God, Whose unsleeping vigilance and power has never for an instant ceased to work for us, to plan for us, to foresee through all the vicissitudes of changing ages the coming of our puny being to earth. Never a moment of those inconceivable reaches of time during which the swirling nebula, which was to be this world, was cooling into shape, during which the stern lines of stubborn rocks were melting into soil and the torrential rains were smoothing the surface of continents, but God was considering with love how He might benefit and bless us on this earth which He was shaping for our good.

THE UPHOLDING OF THE UNIVERSE

God created not only matter itself, but the laws of matter, and He sustains them constantly by His almighty power. Created things have not within themselves the reason for their own existence. They require to be supported by the power of God, or they would fall back again into the nothingness from which they came. Hence, it is true, in a very real sense, that God is constantly working in the universe, maintaining all things in being and order, sustaining all by His almighty power, and that He does this and always has done it out of love for us, whom the whole universe is meant to serve.

Through uncounted ages, God thus worked for us in

His world, making it ready for the coming of man. Moses saw this long process of preparation, perhaps in a series of visions as some scriptural commentators say, and he describes it in Genesis. The findings of geology strikingly bear out his orderly description. First, the earth produced plants, then animals, and last, the king and summit of creation was created by God to possess and rule this marvelous globe. In every forward step of nature, in every new appearance or development of life, it was God Who worked for us with almighty love and goodness, foreseeing our coming needs and making the world fit for our dwelling place.

THE DAYBREAK OF HISTORY

Then came the dawn of human history. The first man and woman, endowed with marvelous powers of body and mind, the most admirable and excellent of God's visible creatures, were placed in the midst of the lovely earth. This complete abode for their intelligent and free natures was given into their care, to be used for His service, that they might praise and serve God and so deserve an everlasting reward with Him in heaven. We know the sequel to the trial which God made of their obedience and fidelity. They fell, and thereby forfeited for themselves and all their progeny those marvelous gifts which God in His goodness had given to all humanity. They were cast out of paradise, but were promised a Redeemer. Then began the wanderings of man on earth—ever hungry for happiness, ever craving for a good beyond his possession, weaving

[51]

his web of joy and misery out of the warp of human circumstance and the woof of human will, and striving for the unattainable until the various tapestry of the history of peoples and nations has been spread on the looms of the changing years and centuries.

Review in memory and imagination that tremendous complexity of human experience, that changing and colorful history of the ages. In every circumstance, God's power, His goodness, and His unfailing care shine out to the eye of faith from human destinies. In spite of the crimes of man, of the fury of human passions, He maintains the currents of life in our race as He keeps the stars constant in their courses. Each child who is born into the world is a new manifestation of the goodness of God, Who does not destroy the children for the sins of their parents but renews, age by age and generation by generation, the freshness of infancy, the hope of youth, the vigor and splendor of maturity.

Man's Primitive Outwanderings

The first tribes of men, who wandered off from the cradle of the human race into new and unknown regions of the earth, found everywhere God's providence awaiting them, His power sustaining and protecting them. He has forever continued the fruitfulness of the soil, the constant succession of the teeming seasons, the suns and rains of every year which bring fertility to the fields. With a restless spirit of adventure, man has pushed into every region of the world, penetrating the most secret valleys, climbing the cloud-piercing hills, blistering under the suns of the tropics, freezing in the polar wastes, and everywhere he has found the protecting and sustaining love of God. Picture to yourself, if you can, the slow swarming of man over the face of the globe. Everywhere the patient pick and shovel of archaeologists uncover the ruins of buried cities, and the dismal treasures of sepulchral mounds, proofs of the inhabitation of the lands by prehistoric races of man. The caverns of the hills, the cliffs where they have perched their high refuges, the pile-borne villages of the Swiss lakes, and the vast ruins of abandoned cities in South America bear witness to the presence and numbers and power of these vanished men and women of long ago. And when the outlines of history become clearer, and we can trace the birth and death of dynasties, the growth of nations, what a pageantry of dim splendor grows on our musings out of the memories and monuments of the past.

Old Tombs of Oldest Kings

Go into the heart of the desert and look at the long line of the Sahara pyramids, "The oldest tombs of the oldest kings on earth." "They had been there as I see them now," says a modern traveller in Egypt, "thirty centuries before Julius Caesar gazed upon them with his hawk eyes wondering at the mystery of this land he had come to conquer." Some years ago the present writer visited the Egyptiological museum in Milan, one of the most interesting and richest in Europe in its collection of the spoils of Egypt's tombs. There, under a glass case, the skin like parchment, the features sharp and dry after four thousand years in the grave, lay the mummy of an Egyptian priest of that distant epoch, his very flesh preserved from corruption by the art of the embalmers who cheated the worms of their food forty centuries ago. Yet, this old citizen of earth looked on his age as the most modern of the centuries, as indeed it then was, and practiced the arts and the worship of his time with the vague knowledge that they in turn had been handed down to him from generations which antedated even his own.

He was a priest, and the rites he practiced bore witness to the unchanging realization of all ages and tribes that a power on high blesses and rules mankind. He gave thanks for benefits to a power greater than himself, knowing perhaps from some vestige of the primitive revelation that there is a God, almighty and merciful, Whose love is above all His works, Who rewards the good and punishes the wicked, and from Whom all good and blessings flow. So did all nations, without a single exception, through all the course of human history worship and adore a power greater than they. They apprehended this power but dimly by the pale light of reason, helped perhaps by some shreds of primitive revelation. Nevertheless, they gave a worship after their own fashion, scorning to be irreligious and never thinking of outraging their reason by denying the existence of the Maker of the world and the Ruler of men.

MIRROR OF HISTORY

The Torrential Nations

Contemplate again the rise and fall of the great peoples of old, of the Chaldeans and the Assyrians, of the Greeks and the Romans, and the Carthaginians, whose splendid cities rose and fell, whose civilizations, with their arts and letters, had their faint beginnings in prehistoric days of simple and primitive labor, their climax in golden ages of luxury and power, and their weakness and fall in the twilight of decline. Each was great and prosperous in its day, and over each the providence of God watched until it had done its appointed task in the family of nations. The millions upon millions of human lives which made up the course of these torrents of human existence, was each the object of solicitude and love on the part of God, and each had its special share of His providence and favor. We can see only the broad outlines of history. It is the tender and detailed kindness of God to every human soul which will stir our admirations and love for all the ages of eternity, when it is revealed to us in heaven.

Of all the great divisions of history, it is in the dealings of God with the chosen people of Israel in the Old Dispensation and with His Christian People in the New Law that we read most clearly of His goodness and lovableness. Of all the mirroring of God in human history, it is here that His attributes of kindness and amiableness shine with greatest clearness to our feeble eyes. The most surpassing historical interest joins in the Old and New Testaments with the most convincing proofs of God's infinite goodness and love. But it would require another volume, or rather, a whole series of volumes, adequately to deal with a theme so splendid and so vast.

CHAPTER V

THE MIRROR OF SCIENCE

"*I* NEVER look into a high powered microscope," declared a scientist to the present writer some years ago, "without wondering how any man can be so blind as to doubt the existence of God. The infinitesimal worlds of cells and tissues which are revealed therein, are so marvelous in the harmony and design which they display, that inevitable logic compels a thoughtful man to acknowledge and to adore their Creator."

He was right, this keen student of nature. The world of scientific study, not alone as pursued by means of the microscope, but through all its intricate processes, reveals so marvelous an order, so complete and wonderful an evidence of design and power, that it should lift every reasonable observer to the knowledge and love of God. The more the wonders of science increase, the more the admirable and tremendous scheme of creation becomes evident, the greater reason we have to praise and reverence Him, Whose handiwork science but partially and faintly traces in each of her discoveries.

THE TRUMPET-TONE OF PAUL

Saint Paul has uttered, in sentences that ring like trumpets, this truth of the witness of visible things to God's power and divinity. "For the wrath of God is revealed from heaven," he says in his epistle to the Romans (i. 17-20), "against all ungodliness and injustice of those men that detain the truth of God in injustice. Because that which is known of God is manifest in them. For God hath manifested it unto them. For the invisible things of Him, from the creation of the world, are clearly seen, being understood by the things that are made; His eternal power also, and divinity; so that they are inexcusable. Because that, when they knew God, they have not glorified Him as God, or given thanks; but became vain in their thoughts and their foolish heart was darkened. For professing themselves to be wise, they became fools."

The indignation of the Apostle of the Gentiles is justly very great against those pagans, who, having before them the wonderful proofs of God's power and divinity, do not believe therein. But what shall we say of those who having seen in nature and science the moving proofs of the goodness and lovableness of God do not love Him? "The devils," said St. Paul, "believe and tremble." But it is the part of a true man to believe and love.

Science—the Handmaid of Love

Indeed, rightly understood, the marvels of science offer us many reasons for loving God as well as for believing in Him. The Creator is made manifest by the wonders of His works. These wonders are revealed more and more through the patient years by the researches of scientific observers, which thus give us constantly more and more reason for loving God. The mirror of science, held up to God as He is manifested in His creation, offers us sublime glimpses of His infinite goodness, of His power and intelligence which are without end. The more we know of God, the more we should love Him, for the infinite goodness and beauty of His uncreated perfection are in themselves irresistible motives for love and should move us, therefore, to love Him more and more as we increase in our knowledge of Him.

Of course, to be supernaturally pleasing to God, our love must be based on supernatural faith and belief in God's revelation. But having come to believe in God through faith in His revealed word, and to love Him as a consequence of that faith and of His grace, we may increase our faith and love alike by the contemplation of His works in the mirror which science holds up toward His infinite perfections. There, His power and wisdom are seen through the veils of His creation, as in a glass, darkly, but seen nevertheless with marvelous and increasing clearness as the discoveries of science lay bare more and more of the wonders of His works. There is nothing, in all the wide universe of scientific discovery, which does not furnish us with a persuasive motive to love God. Science is forever busy weighing, counting, tasting, touching, and seeing what God has invented and made. It originates nothing, save human terms which describe the divine creations and human processes which depend for their success on the laws made by God and on the qualities which He has given to His creatures.

[59]

MIRRORS OF GOD

The Darkness of Hearts

One may indeed ignore the claims of God, and study His works without any reference to Himself, as some scientists have done. We are reminded again of the indignation of St. Paul against those who "are inexcusable. Because that, when they knew God, they have not glorified Him as God, nor given thanks, but became vain in their thoughts and their foolish heart was darkened. For professing themselves to be wise, they became fools." But the number of such scientists is becoming less and less. The logic of cause and effect, and the compelling power of the cumulative evidence for the existence of an all-wise and all-powerful Creator, bid fair to make the open minded among scientists proclaim, as so many of their leaders have done already, the existence of a First Cause for the wonderful universe. This First Cause is God.

But to love God requires a deliberate exercise of our will over and beyond the intellectual conviction of His existence and even of His lovableness. God does not compel our love, because He wishes us to have the merit of loving Him freely. When we come to heaven, and see Him face to face, we shall indeed love Him of necessity and to the full extent of our powers. But in this world, we may love Him as much or as little as we will. If we love Him greatly, we shall receive a great reward for having loved Him freely and with a willing love. We shall do well, then, to use the discoveries of science and the testimony it renders to God, as a means of stirring ourselves to love Him more and more. Let us briefly recall some of the details of the witnesses of science to the power and goodness of God. We may well begin with the constitution of matter itself, which has of late years been so amazingly disclosed to the tireless researches of investigators.

FORMS OF LOVELINESS

Into what forms of beauty has God wrought this material world! Who does not recall the splendor of majestic sunsets and the pure glory of bright dawns, when the golden east grew intolerably bright with the bursting splendor of the sun? The colors of dawns and sunsets result from the action of air and of the vapors of water on the rays of sunlight. The ethereal beauties of the sky are a manifestation of the powers of that matter of which the universe is made.

Consider, too, the loveliness of water in all the forms in which it meets our gaze. Remember the calm bosom of lakes, reflecting the woods and the sky in a glassy mirror; the glory of waterfalls, careering from the cliffs in snowy foam and filling the air with the voices of many waters; the shining brilliance of ice and snow, glittering in glaciers, blazing in the sun as the icebergs float on summer oceans, and whirling in fleecy drifts before the winter's wind. How exquisite a beauty and a strength has this sublime element in the midmost of ocean, when the seas lift before the tempest and hurl their mountainous waves so high that they seem to wash the skies. As we look from the deck of a staggering ship, making its way against the storm with the power of steam, how terrible is the struggle between the elemental fury of the sea and this machine, the work of human hands. Yet it is the power of water, of water hurled in masses of roaring waves, of water, confined in the form of steam within the boiler of the ship, which furnishes both the strength of the ship's engines and the rage of the turbulent ocean.

Universes in Miniature

If we consult the discoveries of science, we find that every particle of matter is as marvelous as the entire universe. The more deeply man penetrates into the secrets of nature, the more cause he finds for wonder and admiration. Each infinitesimal particle of material substance is like a solar system in miniature, where nuclei and electrons take the place of sun and stars, and where these incredibly minute realities race in wide orbits within the circumference of a bit of matter far smaller than the tiniest mote which we see dancing in the sunbeam. Thus, the dust which rises by the side of the road as we race by in our speeding car. has in its every particle small universes with regular orbits of nuclei and electrons, keeping their appointed paths and speeds as faithfully, in obedience to the laws which God has given them, as do the ponderous sun and the serene and faithful stars.

The discoveries of science concerning living things open up to us a yet more amazing universe of wonders. Within comparatively recent times, it has been found as nearly everyone knows, that all living things are made up of tiny

[62]

"The forests are a mist of green-gold leaves, fine and new, like the chased masterpiece of a craftsman in intricate filigree."

(The Forest by Jacob Van Ruisdael)

units of life called cells, infinitesimal bits of matter, each with its own organization and life. In the simplest form of microscopic beings, the whole organism is but one cell, which can nourish itself and propagate its kind. Visible plants and animals are made up of an immense number of such cells, united into organs and tissues, which together carry on the various functions of life. New cells are born and old ones die, while the whole organism continues in existence. It requires the power of compound microscopes to enable the human eye to see these cells, and so their existence was not known until such microscopes were developed. Yet, from the dawn of creation, God's power and love has kept up continuously this marvelous organic life. God has worked, so to say, in the bodies of all living things, continuing the multiplication of cell life, maintaining this astonishing complexity of organism, through all the cycles of plant and animal existence whose long periods are witnessed by the geological records.

THE MARVELS OF PLANTS

The life of plants is a beautiful balance of functions and life processes. As we look at a noble tree in the sunlight, its leafy branches shading the surrounding soil, we little dream, unless we have studied the revealing pages of botany, what intense activity is taking place in those quiet leaves and branches, or what marvelous processes are going on under the influence of the heat and the sunshine. Below ground, the fine roots are drinking water and nourishment from the soil. This water is passing from cell to cell, by a process called osmosis, through the closed cell walls, until it reaches the leaves, which are in fact the stomach of the tree.

The leaves in turn drink through their thousands of tiny mouths or pores the carbon dioxide of the air, and possessing a subtle constituent called chlorophyl, a word of Greek origin meaning "the green of the leaf" which has the marvelous power, in the presence of sunshine, of breaking up the molecules of this carbon dioxide, they set free the oxygen and retain the carbon in new compounds for the nourishment of the plant. Thus, while animals breathe in oxygen and combining it with the carbon in their bodies breathe out carbon dioxide, plants, at least many of them, breathe in carbon dioxide and breathe out oxygen. In this way the great necessary store of oxygen in the air, whereby we live and which we must breathe or perish, is constantly renewed.

This is only one instance of the marvelous balance and harmony of living things, by which they are made to serve for the welfare of man. We depend primarily on the plants for our nourishment, and they break up the soil, take from it and from the air the elements necessary for us, and combine them into complex substances which can be assimilated by our bodies. Were it not for the plants, we should perish miserably, for all the warm-blooded animals and the fishes whose flesh we eat are in turn nourished by plants. Even in the polar regions, where animal food alone is available for man, the animals which he eats have been fed upon plants, or upon other animals which in turn have been nourished upon some form of plant life, perhaps in the depths of the never-freezing oceans.

THE RICH HARVEST OF SCIENCE

These facts are evident enough to every observer. Science has been busy ferreting out the secrets of God's creation and has discovered that the process by which plants nourish our bodies is far more complex and singular than anyone had thought. Besides the obvious elements of nutrition, the proteids or meat and leguminous foods, the carbohydrates or starches and fats, there are in plants substances called vitamines, obscure and delicate compounds present in living organisms, which are necessary, in some imperfectly comprehended way, for growth and life and without which nutrition is impeded and life itself will eventually cease. These elusive constituents are found in plants throughout the earth, so that wherever man goes he is able to procure what is so necessary for his sustenance yet so delicate and slight as to elude, in great part at least, the processes of chemical analysis.

OUR HUMAN MICROCOSM

When we come to consider the human body itself, how its astonishing complexities and singular balance of processes make us wish to love God and give Him praise for the wonders of His creation! If all the rest of His universe is marvelous, it is the human body that God seems to have placed at the climax of His material creation. Every new discovery of science reveals novel depths and heights of

[65]

delicate organization in man's physical constitution, and what we already know of the elements of health makes us wonder how many further discoveries the increasingly delicate and accurate processes of science are still to make in our physical frame. Little by little, the science of medicine has delved deeper and deeper into man's bodily structure and functions. The physicians of old had only a few details of knowledge, which they obtained from the limited observation of their unaided senses. They knew the symptoms of disease, and some remedies which assisted the healing powers of nature. But they had no microscopes, no delicate instruments of measurement, none of the resources of chemical analysis which nowadays have so forwarded the science of medicine.

Modern times have witnessed an immense progress in medical discovery. The circulation of the blood, the cell-structure of all living things, the functions of various organs, hitherto imperfectly understood, and the complexity and uses of bodily secretions, have all been learned in comparatively recent times. Health is a balance of thousands of processes. The body secretes so many different intricate compounds that the memory staggers at their names, each one has some vital function, even in the infinitesimal quantities in which it exists in the human frame.

HEALTH'S DELICATE BALANCES

Our well-being results from the presence of many requisites and the absence of even one will sometimes cause serious illness. The infinitesimal quantity of hydrogen in the blood might seem a negligible element in our health; yet if it varies by what we should call a hair's breadth of quantity, we become unwell. So also the secretion poured into the blood by the pancreas has lately been found to be of such importance, that unless it be present in due quantities the sugar in the blood cannot be eliminated through its use in muscular action and the disease called diabetes results. So also the secretions of the thyroid gland, of the adrenal gland, etc., have been found to play a necessary part in the economy of life, and new discoveries of this sort are constantly coming to notice.

How great and how lovable must be the Creator of all these wonders. If the inventor of one single cure for mortal ills is heralded as a benefactor of mankind and honored with love and remembrance, how should we love Him Who is the Maker and Healer of human nature, Who has put everywhere the elements of man's nourishment and made possible for him to discover the causes of his disease and the cures which nature holds in trust for him.

Man can, moreover, take from other animals what is needed to fortify or even supply for his own physical lacks and weaknesses. By the use of serums, or toxin antitoxins, derived from the blood of animals, he can cure his own ailments, and he can take the secretions of the thyroid, the adrenal, and other glands of brutes and use them to supplement the natural secretions of the human body.

MIRRORS OF GOD

THE HEALING POWER

But more than all the devices of the healing art is the natural power of the human system to recover the delicate balance of health when it is attacked by disease. The white corpuscles of the blood, called leucocytes, can pursue through the tissues the invading microbes which threaten the body, and can seize and consume these dangerous, though microscopically small, invaders. The various organs of the body have an astonishing power to repair themselves and resist even the abuses which we inflict upon them.

Quiet rest in bed is still the most sovereign of all remedies for the sick, as it was in the days of Galen and Hippocrates. This calm and repose, with the shielding of the sick body from hostile outside influences and from sudden changes of temperature and undue exertions, give the natural powers the chance to recuperate, and the healing power of nature herself, best of all physicians, has opportunity to come into beneficent action. "I dress the wounds, and God heals them," was the motto which a great surgeon put above the door of his operating room, and it might well be written wherever medicine or surgery ministers to the ailments of mankind. It is God who is the Supreme Physician, the Healer, as He is the Maker of man. The human body, with all its wonderful organism, is loud in His praise and summons us to love Him.

We have only skimmed the very surface of science, and have left untouched whole reaches of its discoveries. Who shall sum up in a whole volume the lore of geology, with its revelations of the slow processes by which God formed the universe out of chaos? How many millions of years it needed for the earth to become a fit habitation of man, we can only speculate and wonder. How fast or how slow the processes of nature worked in primitive days, we do not properly know. The whole earth is a book in which we can read the majesty and power of God, written in the strata and their fossils, in the shape and substance of mountains, in the contours of continents, and the beds of ocean.

THE LITANY OF SCIENCE

There is the science of insects, entomology, which recognizes some three hundred thousand varieties of that frail and ephemeral life which is more enduring and changeless upon earth than the pyramids of vanished pharaohs. The gossamer creatures which we see floating on the breeze resist in their tribes and generations the destructive forces of nature which pull down the monuments of Caesars and level Tyre and Nineveh to the dust. Not one of these creatures is without the special protection of God, and shows His power and wisdom in the slight constitution of its living body and its ability to propagate its kind through countless generations by reason of the instincts and powers which He has given to its race.

Chemistry, which has to do with the interactions and changes of material substances, has also revealed a world of its own. It is a universe of reactions and combinations between the elements and compounds of the earth, and the deeper it penetrates into the matter of its study, the more it reveals to us the endless power and kindness of God. He has made His universe endlessly interesting and has put within it unlimited opportunities for discovery and research, which give occupation to man's restless intelligence and faculties of observation and so constantly reveal to him, through the unceasing discoveries of science, the goodness and amiability of the infinite Inventor and Fabricator of all.

OUR LITTLE STORE OF LEARNING

Zoology classifies and describes the genera and species of animals, and botany those of plants. Both have grown so great in the bulk of their discoveries, that men have to specialize in some restricted corner of their vast field of learning. After all these years of tireless research, new species are still being found and named. As to the discoveries which concern the organs and functions of these animals, they go on unceasingly, adding to the store of human learning, which still bears so small a proportion to the actual marvels of God's universe.

Biology has to do with the whole range of life, from its microscopic beginnings, from the infinitesimal beings which can swim at ease in the ocean of a water drop, to the ponderous trees and the largest of animal bulks. It tells of the origin of cell from cell, of the endless complexity of the forms of life, and of the organs and processes by which it is carried on. In its field, it also glorifies God in His goodness and power.

In a word, all human science teaches us to love God

and to praise Him. It can only reveal what He has done and what wonders He has put in His world for man to find. It would be proud and unreasonable, indeed, to forget the Maker and wonder at the creature, to overlook the Inventor and marvel at His astonishing works. We should rather lift our hearts to heaven and say, "O God, Whom the constant discoveries of science forever praise and glorify, showing in clearer and clearer light Your goodness and Your wisdom, Your power and Your love, I wish to employ all the soul-stirring marvels of science to praise Your name and to love You more and more. My heart shall rise from these created beauties and find its joy and its rest only in You. I love You, My God, for Your own sake, because You are so good in Yourself and so worthy of all my love. In each new discovery of science I find a new reason for praising and for loving You."

CHAPTER VI

THE MIRROR OF FLOWERS

IT IS spring, sunny, vigorous, wind-tossed spring, wet with soft rains and warmed with sunbeams, and the earth is exulting in flowers. The forests are a mist of green-gold leaves, fine and new, like the chased masterpiece of a craftsman in intricate filigree. The meadows shine with a carpet of silky green, embroidered with pretty blossoms of every hue. Here beds and fringes of gold and there masses of blue as though a morsel of the sky had floated to earth; here the white and pink of a baby's cheek and there the frail, small firstlings of spring pushing up through the lush grasses.

Then there are the flowers of the trees! The apple trees lift their branches like huge chandeliers where the candles are radiant clusters of pinky white bloom, smelling sweet as the roses. The pear trees wave masses of blossoms, thick as curdled cream, with a keen, strange scent that is half pleasant, half painful. The peach tree flowers are already spent, save here and there where a spray of flame burns in the orchard. These immense bouquets of odor and color, the flowering fruit trees, seem to be not of the earth at all, but rather to belong to the scented blossom banks of heaven.

MIRROR OF FLOWERS

IN THE SWEET FORESTS

In the deep woods, another galaxy of floral beauty is tossing on the tree tops or sleeping in the shadows under the venerable bolls of forest trees. The flowers of the trees are silky and strange, of curious shapes, hues, and odors, but each has its own beauty, its own seal of charm and fragrance given it by the loving care of God. The blossoms in the grass are as different as gems; some pale white, like the blood root; some like the dentaria, edged with crimson; others, like the sweet william and the violet, running through a gamut of blues and purples that make a symphony of color on mossy banks or beside purling streams.

As to the flowers of the garden, who can enumerate their kinds and colors? There is a riot of roses on trellises and in rose beds, roses of every size and hue, some yellow as gold, some red as blood, some of dusky crimson like the strong wine from the grape that grows on the slopes of Aetna and Vesuvius, some white as the snow on Alpine summits where the gorgeous flowers of the heights blaze at the edge of glaciers.

THE TRIBE OF LILIES

The whole tribe of lilies, various and beautiful, rival the roses with their pale, pure chalices, with their flame colored corollas, with gold centers spotted as with blood, with red and flaming cup where the sunlight seems turned to opalescent wine, with every marvelous variety of hue wherewith God has colored the chaste symmetry of lily cups. The phlox and hollyhocks, old familiars of homely

[73]

gardens, yielding to the gardener's art a riot of color and contrast of hue that makes them bright in vivid masses in garden plots of every temperate clime, claim an honorable notice in the hierarchy of flowers. So do the family of daisies, from the pink edged *paquerettes* which make spring beautiful in France and England to the great, queenly marguerites that nod in state on courtly lawns and in sheltered greenhouses.

Who is there in the world that does not love flowers? It is part of our nature to exult in their unspoiled beauty. From times before the present memory of man, they have been the symbols of beauty and innocence, the types of honor and glory, and the comparisons of beauty and of holiness. They lend color and joy to feasts, zest to the rejoicings of glad days, and comfort to times of sorrow. Friends send them to friends to express every shade of kindness and sympathy, of rejoicing and sorrow. They are the ornament of altars and shrines, they give more gladness and convey more varied meanings than aught else but words and music, and they are indeed, as we shall see, both words and music, for they sing and tell of the beauty and lovableness of God.

THE MEANING OF FLOWERS

This is in fact the deepest meaning and most precious message of all the flowers, that they can reveal to us so much of the kindness and loveliness of the Creator, Whose wisdom has planned all the flowers, Whose love spreads them so lavishly across the face of all the world for the delight of man. If there are sermons in stones, and books in the running brooks, there are odes and elegies in the flowers. He must be ill attuned indeed to the harmonies of the universe whose heart will not respond to the music of the flowers, whose eyes cannot read in their grace and beauty, their charm and fragrance, the gleams and reflections which they bear of the uncreated Beauty of God.

FLOWERS—GOD'S THOUGHTS

The flowers are the thoughts of God. It is He Who first conceived them, graceful and splendid, with their forms of loveliness and their colors of wonderful beauty. It was He Who planned what each blossom should possess of shape, hue, and dimension, what impression each should make on our delighted eyes. When we look upon the slightest and most fragile blossom, we are contemplating a realized thought of God.

Where did He find the model for their beauty? The artist who paints the flowers imitates or idealizes what he sees. The sculptor who carves the gleaming marble into the likeness of flowers is guided by the treasures of the woods and gardens. But when God planned the flowers, nothing existed save His own infinite being, His essence, Whose nature it is to exist and which, therefore, is from all eternity. God looked into His own essence and beheld that its uncreated beauty and lovableness could be imitated in the fair forms of flowers. He saw that they, also, could be the mirrors of His beauty, the shadows and images of His lovableness. Out of His own being He conceived

[75]

them, and by His limitless power He brought them to be and sustains them constantly in being. They reflect at every moment the beauty, the kindness, and the lovableness of Him Who has given them for our instruction, consolation, and delight.

The Year's Processional

Who can conceive the number, the variety, or the differing charm of earth's flowers? The changing seasons bring to us of this temperate clime a whole procession of blossoms. In the early spring, the snowdrop and the arbutus are found pushing their intrepid buds through the melting snows. Then come all the ephemeral darlings of spring, the sweet little fountains of delight that spring in shadowy woodlands, and the hardier blossoms that stand and gaze upwards, knee high in meadow grass. Next come the various tribes of compositae, the many legions of the daisies and their kin, from the first early sprinkling of field flowers to the heavy headed goldenrods of which some forty species will gild our summer and autumn fields.

Who could enumerate from memory all our native flowers? There are the harebell and the evening primrose that love their own habitat; the one the border of northern lakes, the other dusty roadsides where its yellow bloom cheers the passer-by. There is the clematis that climbs and clings, enriching its host with clouds of white and pleasant bloom. There is the hydrangea, lover of streams, and the water cress, approver of the purest springs with its cool sprays of small white flowers. They are all thoughts of

God made manifest for our profit and delight. They are little mirrors in which we may see, if we will, the boundless beauty, power, and love that wrought their veined beauty, their fragile and perishing loveliness.

Then there are the tribes of water flowers. We know the white lilies that float in snowy purity on the dark bosom of stagnant fens, like a just soul in a fallen world, and the yellow lilies that thrust their red center upward, as though to catch the pouring beams of sunshine. But in the marshes and by river marges, on most lake beaches and by the salty ocean, there are multitudes of flowers which the scientist preserves and classifies by genera and species and which in some novel way, by shape and color, please the thoughtful and observing eye. They are all thoughts of God, made real by His goodness and power.

In Varying Climes

The traveler who has learned the lore of flowers, and can recognize the differences and affinities of the blossoms of different climes is charmed with their harmony and variety wherever he wanders. In our far western land, he finds the flora of the desert, hardy and inured to drought, the gaunt cactus, lifting its bare arms in defiance against the parching sky, yet bursting into marvelous bloom, rich and splendid as the garden roses, the sage brush with its purple flower, symbol of the desert, and a whole pale company of desert blossoms, drinking a vigorous life from the dry soil and parching air. These, no less than the softer blooms of wet lowlands, praise God Who gave them being and keeps them against the burning sun and withering wind.

Each land and each climate has its own flowers, suited to that especial environment in which they spring. The dank tropical forests, heavy with heat and moisture, breed great voluptuous blossoms, richly colored orchids, huge trumpet flowers, blooms that can thrive in the deep gloom of matted branches and under the steaming heat of tropic suns. The high, rare air of mountain summits also has its crown of flowers, hardy and beautiful, which would pine and die in the miasmic atmosphere of tropic jungles, but which love the rare air of the heights and the coolness and the vigor of mountains.

THE ALPINE BLOOM

There is a lovely race of flowers which blooms only on the summits of the Alps, near the line of perpetual snows. To the climber in those brisk altitudes, there come marvelous visions of color, beds of blossoms as bright and splendid in hue as the dyes of oriental tapestries. Red and blue and purple, massed in huge beds of vigorous bloom, these Alpine flowers haunt the lonely wastes of the lofty mountain tops, as though they wished to praise God where none but the eagle can rise and to give their unearthly beauty only to the most daring spirits who can defy the perils of the uttermost heights. The lavish hand of God has made them spring up and flourish where we should expect no flowers.

MIRROR OF FLOWERS

Continent is linked to continent by God's gift of kindred blossoms. One who has grown familiar with our American flora may cross the seas to Europe confident that he will find there a whole array of bloom like unto yet different from the familiar flora of home. Europe wears its rue with a difference; its daisies are like ours yet not entirely alike; its wild roses resemble ours yet are not identical; its buttercups, which with the daisies make the loveliest carpet for its spring, remind one of our own varieties of buttercups, but with subtle diversities. As with the flowers so it is with birds. These winged flowers, the flowers of the air, show the same curious resemblances with our own and the same subtle differences which mark them with a European strain.

Blossoms of Ocean

Even the ocean has its living flowers, blossom-like creatures which the scientists have named after the blooms which they so closely simulate. These sea anemones, sea pinks, and sea dahlias as they have been called are in fact animals, but they so closely resemble flowers that they would lead the unscientific observer of their ocean beds to declare stoutly that he had seen marvelous flowers growing under the surface of the sea. "A mere description," says one writer, "of the varied and marvelous display of color that greets the eye of those who have had the exquisite pleasure of observing these animals in their native haunts, reads like gross exaggeration. Words fail him who would tell of the wonders he has seen. Instinctively, one likens their profusion of color to the colors of the rainbow."

" 'What beautiful flowers!' you would say if you could see these marvelous creations," declares another observer, "in shades of rose, orange, white, and brown, looking like huge carnations with thick stems. There are others, too, whose petals seem to have unfolded, making them look more brilliant and transparent. What marvelous colors they have. It seems as if they had been stolen from the rainbow. No florist could grow flowers with more perfect shadings and markings than these creatures of the sea, in their many shades of red, violet, brown, yellow, and green."

Thus, the most splendid of the flowers are mimicked by these strange living blossom-animals, which bloom in gorgeous colors in the pale, green waters of the shallow seas. "See how God loves His flowers," said an enthusiastic flower fancier not long ago in speaking of these sea anemones, sea pinks, dahlias, and roses, "when He has imitated them in the depths of the sea, so that even the ocean may not lack its blossoms. And if we would but let Him," continued the same simple and poetic soul, "He would make our hearts as lovely as the flowers."

THE ROSE OF THE BLESSED

In fine, flowers are the art of God, His delicate and fragile reminders of the love and beauty which He has in store for us in heaven. Dante has compared the whole company of the elect to a radiant rose of glory, whose living petals are the company of the angels and the saints, whose glowing heart is the humanity of Christ. The saints have loved to contemplate the flowers, walking in quiet gardens where the presence of God was manifest in these precious memorials of His love.

Gazing at even the simplest flower we may indeed make a sublime meditation upon the all-present, the all-powerful, and all-loving Creator of the world. It is He Who has planned and brought to being this exquisite form of light and graceful beauty. From the budding of its rosy perfection to the last unfolding of its petals, His power was active, through the orderly and beautiful forces of nature, to bring this symmetry and charm to the eyes of men. The regular and varied grace of its contour is the expression of the mind of God, which from all eternity, through inconceivable ages, has planned to bring it to be at this moment for your delight. The power of God keeps it unwithering and serene for this brief instant of time, that it may bring its message of love to your mind and your heart. Slight in its substance, destined only to blossom for an hour and then disappear, the flower at which you are gazing tells you of the brevity of human beauty and delight, and bids you raise your mind and heart to God. But, little and frail as this blossom is, no power save an infinite power could have wrought it, no wisdom save an infinite wisdom could have conceived it. With unfailing authority, it points the finger of its slight being up to God.

In the least of earth's flowers God's beauty is reflected and shadowed, His power shown, His endless love demonstrated to the hearts of men. Let us be glad for the mirror of the flowers, and never fail to see in their frail glasses, held up to heaven, the lovely image of the endless Beauty and Love.

CHAPTER VII

THE MIRROR OF GREAT SOULS

WE CAN see God mirrored all about us, and can learn of His infinite beauty, perfection, and lovableness from any creature. The pebbles and the stars alike teach us something of their Maker. In them we can see dimly, as in an imperfect glass, the lineaments of God. As creatures ascend in the scale of being, they show more and more of the traits, so to say, of Him Who invented and made them. Thus, the inanimate world tells much about God but less than the world of living things. In turn, the whole world of living things cannot reveal to us so much about God as can man, His masterpiece in the visible creation, the apex of the pyramid of sensible beings, the image of God both in his soul and in his body, but especially in his soul.

DIFFERENCES OF RESEMBLANCE

Even among men, as we ascend through the strata of human character, we find some individuals far surpassing others in their capacity to reveal to us, by their own excellence and lovableness, the amiability and perfection of their Creator. Even the lowliest mortal has in him something Godlike, because he has an intelligence and free will which are a limited copy of God's endless intelligence and freedom. Just as we have many pictures of our national heroes, some far better than others but all possessing a certain resemblance, having at least human lineaments and the general shape of a man, so also all men and women are images of God. Some resemble Him merely in that they have intelligence and free will, which they abuse so as to distort and mar the likeness of God within them, while others wonderfully conform themselves to the goodness and kindness of God by being good and kind, and by using their Godlike faculties of intelligence and free will to become noble themselves and to ennoble all over whom they have an influence.

Thus, while to the thoughtful and open mind all men mirror God's lovableness, the finer and greater souls marvelously excel in shadowing forth to us His indescribable and endless perfection. Reflecting on the charming nobleness and goodness of these great souls as we know them, our hearts are lifted up to contemplate the infinite perfection of their Creator, and to love Him Whom we see from these admirable images of His goodness to be so worthy of love.

A Salutary Thought

It is good for us to recur again and again to the thought that all men, like the whole remainder of creation, are the work of God. He planned them in His eternity, created the material out of which their bodies are formed at the commencement of the world, and brought them to be in accordance with His natural laws, creating and breathing into their bodies a new and immortal soul at the moment of their conception, the first instant of their individual life.

There is no comparison which is strong enough to convey to us how utterly all men are the work of God, the possession of God, how He deserves, so to say, the credit for whatever good they are, or have, or do. He has planned them, made them, and He keeps them in being. They are utterly incapable of doing the least good unless He aids and supports them by His endless power. As we came from nothingness by the power of God, so it is He alone Who keeps us from tumbling back into that native nothingness. Our whole physical being rests on Him as its Creator and Sustainer, the source and support of all.

Delusive Self-Sufficiency

We may seem self-sufficient and able to continue our little life of our own strength, for a while at least, but this is only seeming. Our reason tells us that if we could not emerge out of nothing by our own power, neither can we continue to exist thereby. It is the unseen God (unseen as we have explained, by reason of the feebleness of our faculties, not because of any imperfection on His part), Who keeps us in being and gives us constantly all that we possess.

Therefore, whatever of goodness and nobleness we possess is the property of God more than our own. We are not only images of Him, but all our goodness is referable to Him. Great souls not only reflect His perfections, they are the consequence, so to say, of His goodness. In studying them, we behold the most splendid examples within our ken of the handiwork of the Most High. The great souls who are the heroes of our human race stir us to wonder, admiration, and sometimes to love, when we read their lives, study their exploits, and realize their sublime achievements.

THE SPLENDOR OF GENIUS

In its highest reaches, the grandeur of the human intelligence is sublime. Such minds as Dante and Shakespeare, men whose genius seems almost superhuman, have left behind them in their works the record of their great thought. In his astounding trilogy, the Inferno, the Purgatorio, and the Paradiso, Dante has reached the mountain tops of achievement of the creative imagination. He has conceived a new heaven and a new earth, piercing with his poetic vision the inner recesses of human nature and leaving in immortal verse the record of conceptions so sublime that they seem the work of some poet among the angelic hierarchies.

So does the genius of Shakespeare, quite different in kind from that of Dante, astonish the student of his works. His knowledge of human nature was so profound, his insight into human motive and character so subtle and various, that it is hard to conceive how his faculties could achieve a task so extraordinary. Yet his works bear the evidence of an unstudied ease which sometimes forms a strange contrast to his exalted art. These men are master-

"The flooding sunshine, searching out all the world and bathing it in light, warmth, and vigor, symbolizes God's universal beneficence which reaches to all the uttermost parts of His creation and preserves in being every creature which He has made."

(Landscape by Jacob Van Ruisdael)

pieces of God's hands, and their intelligence and creative power are a faint indication of His own.

GREAT SOULS OF SCIENCE

So too are the great souls of science, those subtle observers, those ingenious theorists, who with their five weak senses and their untiring minds have pushed back little by little the frontiers of human knowledge into the domain of scientific discovery. Euclid and Archimedes, in mathematics, Galen and Hippocrates in medicine, Socrates, Aristotle, and Plato in pure mental philosophy, were minds which originated modern science and with the pure genius of the Greeks gave the tone to the thought of following civilizations. They also were the work of God and owe all their sublime power to His sustaining hand.

The leaders of modern research give no less glory to God by their achievements than did those ancient pioneers of learning. When Harvey discovered the circulation of the blood, it was but one creature of God, intelligent and free, discovering another of God's creative achievements. When Newton first formulated the laws of gravity, he gave another instance of human genius, another reason for loving God. Scientists have sometimes been the first to give praise to God for His wonderful works when they found out some new instance of His goodness. But whether or not they acknowledge and give praise to their Creator, they remain none the less the creatures of His hands, dependent on Him for all things, for life, for reason, for the very existence which they possess.

MIRRORS OF GOD

The Sagacity of Rulers

The genius of rulers and the power they had to sway and govern the turbulent multitudes of mankind, were owed to God. Caesar and Alexander, men with whose names we conjure up the splendor of ancient empires based on conquest, were as utterly God's doing, as the most insignificant insect. The keen intellect with which they studied the manners and motives of men, so as to sway and control the peoples over which they ruled, gives us a faint hint of God's overruling wisdom. They dimly image, in their small mirrors, the unending light of God's intelligence.

But more sublime than human intelligence is the moral grandeur of the human will. Great intellect can go hand in hand with great villainy, as history too often witnesses with sorrow. Intelligence is a gift which does not primarily depend on our own efforts or choice. Some men are dowered by nature with keen intellect and quick comprehension, with accurate judgment and close deduction. But the will of man is his own, to better and to perfect. His moral nature is under his own sway and whether it be good or evil depends on his own free actions. So, by common consent, moral greatness is far superior to high intelligence. When we come to know of some one whose intellect is very keen we may admire and wonder, but we love those whom we perceive to be great in their goodness and their power of will.

MIRROR OF GREAT SOULS

GREAT MYTHS AND HISTORIES

Ancient times had many a tale, some true and some mythical, of the courage of warriors and the self-sacrifice of patriots. As you walk through the Roman Forum, that wonder place of history and legend, where so much took place that is a part of the story of our whole race and has influenced the course of all succeeding generations, you may see the spot where, according to the ancient legend, Quintus Curtius spurred his steed into the yawning chasm and appeased the anger of the gods of Rome. You may look upon the supposed foundations of the house of Numa Pompilius, a type of the early kings of that frugal realm which sent forth its undaunted legions to conquer the world.

From this storied forum, Scipio the Delayer set forth to foil the victorious armies of Hannibal by his patience. Here, all the real and fabulous heroes of Rome built up that tradition of moral greatness which sustained a tottering empire for so many centuries. These great souls, the historic heroes and those among the mythical figures who were real men but are now seen through the enlarging and distorting mists of years, were all the works of God and all manifest in their own way His perfections and lovableness. Whatever they had in their hearts of nobleness and courage, in their souls of magnanimous strength, was the gift of God and the image of His greatness.

MIRRORS OF GOD

The Most Heroic Romans

Look across the Roman Forum towards the vast circle of the Hadrian amphitheatre, that Colosseum where in imperial times the crowds of Rome assembled to witness the bloody deaths of the Christian martyrs, and you shall evoke the memories of still more heroic Romans. Let us wander thither in fancy and stand in the great arena on which the tiers of arches still look down as they looked of old, in the days of the Caesars. Here, on the smooth sands which hid the cages of fierce beasts and the runways from which they sprang to bite and slay, stood, time and again, groups and throngs of men, women, and children ready and glad to die for the faith of Christ. They came from every class and station which that immense empire had gathered into its all-devouring bulk. Some were great nobles of Rome, patricians whose hereditary name and possessions put them at the summit of the world. Some were slaves, sprung of barbarous peoples, their spirit broken by subjection and toil, their backs marked by the lash, and their souls scarred with the ignominy of slavery. Some were strong men, warriors, used to look death in the face unflinchingly on bloody fields of war. Others were children, girls whose frail bodies shuddered at the sight of the lions springing forth to devour them but whose souls possessed a strange, heroic courage, born of the Spirit of God which dwelt in their hearts.

These Christian martyrs in the primitive days of faith present the most sublime, most touching, and wonderful

example of great-souled courage in the midst of fear-
inspiring surroundings. Weak though they were, they
dared the whole terrible power of the Roman *Imperium,*
that strong, relentless system which could stretch its armed
hand to the farthest quarters of the world and inflict on
those who had offended against its laws the most brutal
tortures of that ruthless time. It had enslaved whole peoples, had imposed its laws on the most diverse nations, and
had grown so great in power that it was truly the mistress
of the world.

DESPITE ROME'S MAJESTY

Yet, these weak and helpless individuals, facing the
organized strength of Rome, defied with calm and deter-
mined courage all the blandishments and the threats of the
Roman judges, all the hideous tortures of the Roman executioners. It was God within their hearts that nerved them
to withstand so terrible a pressure of power which urged
them to deny Christ and His teachings, inviting them with
bland promises to offer incense to the Roman gods. The
number of these martyrs is astonishing. They died, not by
tens and hundreds but by hundreds and thousands, nay, by
hundreds of thousands. For the most part, their very names
are unknown to us, but the precious annals of those times,
all too scant and few, preserve nevertheless some bright
instances of their words and actions in the face of so dreadful a death for their faith.

There was that Bishop, who, brought before the judge
on the charge of being a Christian, confessed his faith

with such joy and courage that the Roman magistrate eagerly desired to win him to sacrifice to the Roman gods and give his allegiance to the false religion of that mighty empire. This magistrate summoned the executioners before the judgment seat and bade them exhibit to the calm eyes of the martyr all their dreadful array of fiendish instruments of torture. There was the rack with its cunning devices of ropes and pulleys, to tear joint from joint and strain the tortured ligaments until they burst; there was the wheel, to break bones and lacerate the quivering flesh; there were claws and hooks of steel to scarify the limbs with bloody wounds; there was the dreadful gridiron, on which, stretched over a smouldering fire, the martyr would endure an eternity of slow torment before life was driven from his parched and crusted limbs. All these were displayed on one side of the tribunal.

The Riches of Empire

On the other side the judge bade his minions exhibit all the wealth of gold and jewels which he could gather. There were rich stuffs of Tyrian dye, the beautiful purple fit for the garments of kings; there were gems from India and gold from provinces. The splendor and luxury of the richest empire on earth was shadowed forth in those luxurious ornaments. Then, the judge made a last effort to break the constancy of the martyr. "Look," he said, "upon these instruments of torture and behold what you shall receive if you persist in following Christ. Look then upon all of this wealth and splendor, and know that you shall have it all, and more besides, together with great dignity in the state if you forswear Christ and offer incense to the gods of Rome."

WHY THE HERO WEPT

The martyr looked upon the one and the other, the wealth of Rome and her dreadful torments, and then saying no word he began to weep. "Why are those tears," said the judge, "if you fear so much, make your decision quickly. You have no cause to weep when the wealth and honors of Rome lie at your feet." "I do not weep for fear," replied the martyr, "because I am glad to suffer all your tortures for the love of Christ. Rather, I weep to think that these tawdry riches and honors, your bits of stone and metal, and your robes of the wool of sheep should be set off against the sweet love of Christ. I weep that you should dream for an instant that the honor and wealth of Rome could turn me away from Him Who is my Savior and my God."

THE ACTS OF MARTYRS

Such instances of sublime moral greatness abound in the Acts of the Martyrs, those brief and touching histories in which antiquity has handed down to us the words and deeds of those who died for Christ. In such moral greatness is gloriously mirrored the majesty and power of God, Who can so wonderfully strengthen the human heart and ennoble the human will. If His creatures can rise to so triumphant a height of moral strength and dignity, how lovable must be the uncreated God Who has brought them all into being and Who sustains by His mighty power the greatness of their souls. Thus, the characters and exploits of the martyrs are a beautiful mirror of God. From the holy shades of the catacombs and from the simple inscriptions on the martyrs' tombs there shines the light of God's greatness and goodness. The venerable round of the Hadrian amphitheatre, the old stones of the lately excavated Forum, and the roads that run from Rome over the waste Campagna are so many reminders of that race of early Christians, who lived and died in splendid fidelity to the faith and who left to all the ages their witness to the God Who made them.

This moral greatness of the early Christians was but an imitation and reflection of the soul of the Founder of Christianity, Who in His single self, and in the dignity and beauty of His human nature, is the sublimest of all mirrors of God's perfection. It was from Him, the Christ, their Teacher and Savior, that His Apostles learned the moral heroism which sent them to die the death of martyrs. Only St. John, who was indeed plunged into a caldron of boiling oil outside the Latin Gate and thus received the merit of martyrdom, was miraculously delivered from that death. It was from Christ that this whole throng of martyrs, men and women, boys and girls, the tender and the weak as well as the mighty and the old, learned the secret of sublimest courage which sent them to die for their faith on the bloody arena.

MIRROR OF GREAT SOULS

Our Richest Age

No age is so rich as our own in the proofs and examples of God's greatness and goodness. Few of us indeed have ever sounded the depths of that saying. Ours is the heritage of the years, the long series of human history from the beginning until our day. The records of remote ages have been searched for our instruction and the glorious traditions of the past have been written anew into modern speech for our edification. The researches of science have unearthed for us wonder after wonder of God's creation. We have more reasons for loving God, more means of knowing Him, and more various and wonderful witness to His power and goodness than the people of any other age have ever possessed.

Means, moreover, for utilizing to our own advantage this rich heritage of the past, were never so abundant as today. Books may be had everywhere, the shelves of great libraries groan with volumes, which will tell us of the wonders of science and of the great episodes and figures of human history. Knowledge was never more diffused than now, science never more developed, thought never more easy of access, education never more general or free. Do we then love God as we should in the midst of this abundance? Do we behold Him and learn of His excellences and perfections, when the whole universe is forever holding up to our eyes innumerable mirrors, each one reflecting something of His surpassing beauty, wisdom, and power? Or does the very multiplicity of God's gifts obscure the

Giver? Are we so interested in creatures which He has made that we fail to worship the Creator? Are we like children, playing with toys, who think only of the pleasant moment and destroy precious and beautiful things regardless of the true purpose for which each was made?

We are rebuked by the moral grandeur of the martyrs. The world of their time was as dear to them as is ours to us. The ties of family were as strong in their breast as in ours. Their flesh shrank from the teeth of lions, from the tearing of the instruments of torture, and from the rack and the flame as ours would shrink. Yet, they endured all, sacrificed all, and rejoiced in all, for the single faith, hope, and love they had in God. They are mirrors of God's holiness and beauty; they are examples, likewise, of the love and service we should render to that Uncreated and Infinite Goodness and Love.

CHAPTER VIII

THE MIRROR OF CHRIST'S HUMANITY

*T*HOUGH THE entire universe shines with the lovableness of God, and mirrors back the beauty and amiability of Him Who brought it out of nothing and planned it according to His own infinite goodness, it remains true that the loveliness of God is reflected in different ways and various degrees by the mirror of His creatures. We see God as in a glass or mirror, darkly, says St. Paul, in this exile from our Father's home. When we are members of His household of heaven, we shall see Him face to face and shall know Him even as we are known.

THE HARVEST OF REVERENT MINDS

A reverent and seeking mind may read God's attributes reflected on all the fair face of creation. The smiling meadows, heavy with ripe wheat, hint to us of the infinite generosity of Him Who feeds the least of the sparrows, and has pity on the smallest, as well as on the greatest of His creatures. The splendid and serene outlines of lofty mountains, towering into the sky, rooted so firm in earth that they have withstood the quakings and storms of centuries, indicate to us the strength of God and His unchanging being.

The flooding sunshine, searching out all the world and

bathing it in light, warmth, and vigor, symbolizes God's universal beneficence which reaches to all the uttermost parts of His creation and preserves in being every creature which He has made. The terrible voice of the storm, the crackling of the lightning, and the sonorous thunder tell of the power and the wrath of God which can smite the mighty oaks of the forest and splinter their rude branches, or can shatter the stony summits of the mountains and send the cringing avalanches rolling down before the power of His arm.

The winds, in their mighty sweep over the face of the world, remind us of the ever-present power of God which touches all creation as the air, fluid and mighty, embraces and moves the surface of the world. The soft voice of zephyrs in the trees and the loud roar of irresistible tempests are alike a mirror of the presence of God in this world, rewarding and punishing, moving and directing through the power of the Spirit, Who came upon the Apostles in the form of tongues of fire and with a noise as of the rushing of a mighty wind.

ALL LIVING THINGS

All the living things on the face of the world remind us, as we have said, of the beauty, the power, the kindness, and the lovableness of their mighty Creator. The smallest of created things, the single cells, which live a microscopic life on land and water, in a world which man has but recently been able to penetrate with the aid of high powered microscopes, proclaim the endless truth of God's infinite amiableness. The smallest of visible things, the infinitesimal plants and animals that float in the currents of ocean or live in sluggish streams wandering over the fields of earth, are each so perfect a creation that their tiny microcosms speak of God to the understanding heart as eloquently as the circling stars. The mosses, clinging to forest trees, and the hidden flowers that blossom in the grass are each a world in miniature and none but an all-wise, an all-powerful, an all-kind, and lovable God could have brought the least of them to be, or could sustain them for an instant in their being.

The whole world of living things which have sense and motion are even more eloquent of their Creator. The sinuous beasts of the tropic jungle, the hardier fauna of our temperate clime, and all the beasts that live and thrive in unhunted forests, also proclaim the lovableness of God. They are all inventions of His wisdom, achievements of His creative power, sustained by His mighty hand, and guided by the unerring instincts which He has given them. The huge and cunning elephant, which crashes its burly way through the thick tangle of tropic woods and the timid field mouse, which hides beneath the corn blade and nurses its quivering young under the shadow of a leaf of burdock, are equally the work of God.

THE TRIBES OF MEN

When we come to the swarming populations of mankind, we find in them far more vivid and accurate mirrors of the beauty and lovableness of God. Man is the most perfect image of God in all the visible creation. Not only his bodily frame, but especially the substance and the faculties of his soul are made to God's image and likeness. He is the link between the world of matter and of spirit, joining the visible creation with the choirs of angels through his spiritual nature and his supernatural destiny. He has intelligence and free will. His intelligence is modeled after God's own intelligence, whereby he can know and discern the truth from falsehood, right from wrong. This lordly gift of intelligence, possible only to a spiritual nature, makes man an incomparably more perfect mirror of God than all the rest of the visible creation together. But greater and more godlike than the gift of intelligence is the splendid faculty of the free will, which makes man most like to God because it enables him to choose or to refuse, to take one course rather than another, to resist the thrust of circumstance, and to strive on with heroic perseverance against obstacles which seem overpowering. The moral heroism of man, when it is put forth to accomplish the will of God and to fulfill justice, is the sublimest and most Godlike attribute of human nature, mirroring for us the greatness and goodness of the infinite Creator of Whom man is the handiwork and the masterpiece.

The Peerless Christ

Yet, all these mirrors of God dwindle into utter littleness as a means of knowing and loving God compared to the human nature of Jesus Christ. In giving to the world

His only begotten Son, made man, to be our Savior, our Teacher and Example, God has offered to us a mirror of His own divine perfections and lovableness which is incomparably more precious than all the rest of the universe together, even than the multitudinous tribes and families of man. In Christ, we shall find visible the beauty and lovableness of the uncreated God. In Him shines forth the amiableness of the divinity cloaked, it is true, beneath the veils of our humanity, but beaming forth with a convincing power to all who have eyes to see and hearts to love.

From the beginning man has yearned, sometimes with a half-conscious yearning, to know more of the hidden and invisible God. Fretted by their own imperfections, which kept them from knowing God more perfectly, the philosophers and poets of bygone ages in pagan lands have strained every faculty of their spirit to show forth under human form the splendor of the divinity. The mythologies of pagan nations were desperate and eager efforts to express the attributes of God under human forms and in human languages.

The primitive revelation of the oneness of God and His supreme and singular dominion was clouded over by the dreams of poets or the fancies of pagan priests. Every race made for itself legends and traditions concerning gods and goddesses whose adventures and exploits, though sometimes strangely fantastic and wild, still expressed the strivings of fallen and darkened human minds to body forth the Infinite in terms of human speech.

The nations of the north conjured up the sparkling and spacious dwellings of Walhalla, where Odin, Thor, and Baldur, and all their glittering court fought and feasted in an endless series of battles and revels which embodied the ruddy and bold genius of those northern nations.

POETIC GREECE

The subtle mind of Greece, shaping the rough-hewn legends of earlier days, carved therefrom the classic mythology of the ancients, with its beautiful and tragic stories, its personification of the elemental powers, and its expression of the struggles of the human soul with fate and the overruling power of the gods. The wide spreading heavens became the great god Jupiter, father and ruler of Olympus. The other powers of nature were typified by other gods and goddesses. The attributes of the Most High were personified in anthropomorphic deities and these again were multiplied by poetic imaginations of Roman times. Every wood had its guardian spirit and every hearth its Lares and Penates; the forests were filled with fauns and dryads, and the streams and oceans with nymphs and tritons, beautiful but futile efforts of the yearnings of poets to express the inexpressible and unknowable God.

Then came the sad delusion of paganism when men worshipped these false deities, the creations of their own fancy, and forgot the one God Who had given their forefathers the primitive revelation of His truth. The speculations of man concerning the nature and attributes of God became more and more clouded and bewildered.

"All the living things on the face of the world remind us of the beauty, the power, the kindness, and the lovableness of their mighty Creator."

(Landscape with Mill by Claude de Lorraine)

Only certain great philosophers, like Plato, Socrates, and Aristotle reasoned rightly and truly, according to their limited comprehension, concerning the one God Who is the Creator and Ruler of the universe. Even they knew but little about the mercy and goodness, the kindness and lovableness of the Most High.

IMAGINED DEITIES

In every nation the imaginations of men made gods according to their own desires. The lands of the orient sprouted a whole hierarchy of strange gods and goddesses. The dreamy followers of Brahma, passing from the monotheism of their ancestors into a strange pantheism, longed to lose their own individuality and to be absorbed into a great world spirit. The people, dissatisfied with this impersonal deity, made many gods of their own, such as Siva the destroyer, Rudra the storm king, Vishnu the genial god of the sun, and other gods and heroes which multiplied almost without end.

Meanwhile, the Jews kept alive in the world the pure doctrine of one God, supreme, almighty, and all-knowing. Yet, even they had only an imperfect knowledge of God's lovableness as compared to the wonderful light and consolation brought to us by Christ. When the fullness of time had come, the heavenly Father had pity on the ignorance and darkness of mankind. He bade His only begotten Son, the Word of the Father, coequal and eternal with Himself, to take a human nature and to come upon earth as one of our brethren, like unto ourselves in all things, except sin, that looking upon Him we might see God clothed in our own flesh and learn from Him as from a most perfect mirror what are the depths and heights of the kindness, the mercy, the tenderness, and the sweetness of the all-lovable and all-loving God.

FABLES OF GODS AND MEN

The mythologies of old dreamed of gods who came down from heaven and walked familiarly with men. The legends of Greece and of Rome abounded with the stories of Jupiter and Mercury, of Venus and Minerva, consorting with mankind. The adventures of the young Krishna in Brahminical mythology are full of similar tales of the all too-intimate dealings of their imaginary god with men. But even the most beautiful of these legends pale into insignificance before the simple and true story of Christ, and many of them are revolting in the extreme in their tales of the evil-doing of these imaginary deities.

The Incarnate Son of God came upon earth to win men's hearts and to establish a kingdom of love, of willing service, of brotherly charity, and of the faithful imitation of mankind of the goodness and lovingness of God. God's love and God's lovableness shine out irresistibly in all the details of His life and His death and in all the traits of His character. He came not to crush nor to punish, but to comfort and save. He came, not to avenge on man the sins of mankind, but to take upon Himself the awful penalty of our guilt and to save us from the consequences of our own misdoings. The most lovable and the most loving of all the sons of men, He draws us irresistibly if only we will yield to His influence and follow His leadership toward the love of God for His own sake and will love all our fellowmen for the sake of God.

CHRIST'S GREAT COMMAND

"A new commandment I give unto you," He said to all His followers, "that you love one another, as I have loved you, that you also love one another. By this shall all men know that you are My disciples, if you have love one for another." This He said in His last discourse to His apostles, and He added, "This is My commandment, that you love one another, as I have loved you. Greater love than this no man hath, than a man lay down his life for his friends" (St. John xiii. 34-35 and xv. 12-13).

When one of the Pharisees, a doctor of the law, asked Him, tempting Him: "Master, which is the great commandment in the law?" He took occasion of this subtle questioning to synopsize all His teaching in two commandments which should be written deep in all human hearts. Jesus said to him: "Thou shalt love the Lord thy God, with thy whole heart, and with thy whole soul, and with thy whole mind. This is the greatest and the first commandment. And the second is like to this: Thou shalt love thy neighbor as thyself. On these two commandments dependeth the whole law and the prophets" (St. Matthew xxii. 37-40).

We, who are steeped in Christian thought and Christian teaching, find it difficult to realize the profound

[105]

change made in the hearts of individuals and nations by the teaching of Christ concerning the love of God and the love we owe to God and to man for God's sake. Even those unhappy groups, and individuals who have rebelled from the authority of Christ and repudiated His teaching, are yet profoundly moved by the moral atmosphere which Christianity has brought into the world. The vast works of charity which we see today, supported alike by believer and non-believer, are the result of Christ's teaching and would have been impossible without His influence.

THE FOUNT OF CHARITY

Before He came, men hated strangers, they despised the poor, and they were coldly indifferent to the sufferings of men and women who had no ties of kindred with themselves. Even the book of Leviticus in the Old Testament gives the commandment, "Thou shalt love thy friend as thyself" (Leviticus xix. 18). It was needful for our Lord to say in His sermon on the mount, "You have heard that it hath been said, thou shalt love thy neighbor, and hate thy enemy. But I say to you, Love your enemies: do good to them that hate you: and pray for them that persecute and calumniate you; That you may be the children of your Father Who is in heaven, Who maketh His sun to rise upon the good and bad, and raineth upon the just and the unjust. For if you love them that love you, what reward shall you have? do not even the publicans this? And if you salute your brethren only, what do you more? do not also the heathens this? Be you therefore perfect, as also your heavenly Father is perfect" (St. Matthew v. 43-48).

Through the study of the words and the actions of Christ, through the thoughtful consideration of His teaching, we may learn more of the lovingness and lovableness of God than in all the books of the universe, all the wonder of the stars, the beauty of the earth, the splendor of the seasons, and the goodness and the nobleness of human kind. Christ in His divinity is the perfect image of His Father, shining back eternally all the perfection of the uncreated deity, true God of true God, Light of Light, begotten, not made, consubstantial with the Father, in all eternity. In His human nature, Christ is also a most pure and perfect mirror of God's benignity and goodness, His mercy and loving kindness, His amiability and love. The uncreated deity we cannot see, but we can study the lineaments of Christ and learn therefrom the beauty of God Himself. For ages humanity has desired to see God, to know God as He is, to be like unto God, but who, even of the most daring of poets, the most keen of philosophers, the most aspiring of sages of pagan times ever dreamed or aspired to see God in the flesh, to hear His words in the human voice, to look into the face of one who is, at the same time, true God and true man, God from all ages of ages and Man from the fullness of time when the Word was made Flesh and dwelt amongst us.

MIRRORS OF GOD

The Mirror of the Father

In the sweet intimacy of the discourse to His disciples,
at the last supper, Christ bade them believe in Him and
see mirrored in Him the lineaments of His Father. "Let
not your heart be troubled," He said to them, "you believe
in God, believe also in Me * * * I am the Way, and
the Truth, and the Life. No man cometh to the Father,
but by Me. If you had known Me, you would without
doubt have known My Father also: and from henceforth
you shall know Him, and you have seen Him."

The hearts of His apostles wondered at this word.
They did not yet realize how perfectly Christ is a mirror of
His Father, how wonderfully he who beholds even the
human nature of Christ which is substantially united to
the divinity beholds a perfect image of the beauty and
the lovableness of God. It was Philip who expressed both
the yearning of their hearts and their lack of comprehension. "Philip saith to Him: 'Lord show us the Father, and
it is enough for us.'" The question wounded the loving
Heart of Christ and drew from Him a protest and an
explanation. "Jesus saith to Him: 'Have I been so long
a time with you; and have you not known Me?'" He
grieved at the lack of understanding of these poor men
who had associated intimately with the Word of God
made Flesh, and had not perceived that in knowing Him
they had known the very God Himself, the perfect mirror
of His Father. Then He makes this clear to them by
words that admit of no mistaking their meaning. "Philip,"

He says, "he that seeth Me seeth the Father, also. How sayest Thou, show us the Father? Do you not believe that I am in the Father and the Father in Me? The words that I speak to you, I speak not of Myself. But the Father Who abideth in Me, He doth the works" (St. John xiv. 1-10). What an invitation to study the beauty of God in the beauty of Christ, the lovableness of God in the lovableness of Christ. Knowing Him we shall know the Father. We shall see the beauty of the Father mirrored in His humanity.

CHAPTER IX

THE MIRROR OF CHRIST'S YOUTH

*B*EFORE THE coming of the Incarnate Son of God, many were the dreams of the poets concerning the manner in which a god would come and walk among men in case He so condescended to seek to win their friendship and their love. The framers of these legends had not indeed an adequate notion of the true dignity and majesty of the Eternal and Infinite God. Their ideas of God had already departed far from the primitive revelation made to Adam, and even the pure light of human reason no longer revealed to them, as it did to the greatest philosophers of pagan times, the nature and majesty of God. For them, therefore, that a god should descend on the earth and walk among men, meant only that one of their half-human deities with a human form and alas, too often, with human passions and vices, should come among men with preternatural powers and added dignity, but with no great difference from the human folk among whom he walked and with whom he dwelt.

WEAVERS OF MYTHS

Thus the classic adventures of Jupiter and Apollo, of Juno, Mercury, Minerva, Venus, and Mars, and all the court of Olympus, were merely poetic imaginings concerning half-human gods and goddesses, whose condescension in visiting the kings and heroes of earth, was not so very much greater than if a king had deigned to descend from his regal state and consort with the ordinary people of his kingdom. In imagining the adventures of these gods among men, the weavers of classic mythology gave indeed human characteristics and human feelings to their deities, but they never conjectured truly what would happen if the one true God should come down upon earth and walk among men.

Their gods and goddesses never assumed the burdens and sufferings of human nature, never immolated themselves for the welfare of mankind. They had sometimes beautiful and sometimes sordid adventures; they exercised their preternatural powers for and against mankind; they did good things and evil, as men might do in similar circumstances. The notion that the eternal God, infinite, perfectly happy, sufficient of Himself in all things, separated by an endless chasm of superior being from the greatest of mankind, should descend to earth, become a man, make Himself like unto us in all things except sin, and then live and suffer and die for our salvation, was a thing beyond their wildest fancies or their sublimest dreams.

The Dreams of Jews

Even the Jews, with all the prophecies to help them, with all the tremendous thunders of Isaias ringing in their ears, with the vivid picturings of David, with the wailings

[111]

of Jeremias and his lamentations over the sorrows which
Israel would bring upon her God, made man, with the
visions of Ezekiel, the startlingly definite promises of
Daniel, with the expostulations of Micheas, the warnings
of Joel, the exhortations of Sophonias, had conceived no
adequate notion, for the most part, of how the Son of God,
the only begotten of the Father, was to become Flesh and
dwell among them. Their idea of the Messianic kingdom
was of a temporal empire, of world-wide majesty, when
the Messiah was to sit on the throne of David, ruling in
wealth and glory all the nations of the earth made subject
to His sway. Even Christ's apostles, to the very time of
His passion, still kept their hopes and dreams of this
earthly kingdom of Israel in which their Master was to be
King and they the princes of His court.

They asked Him, time and again, "Lord, wilt Thou
at this time, restore the kingdom of Israel?" (Acts i. 6).
The mother of the sons of Zebedee begged that her two
dear children should sit at His right hand and His left
in the glory of His kingdom. It was the almost universal
expectation of the Jews, in which the very apostles shared,
that Christ, when He came, would be a mighty and fortu-
nate Prince in Israel, the Ruler and Lord of an earthly
and world-embracing monarchy. Even the wisest of mankind, had he known the dignity and holiness of God and
become aware that this infinite God was to descend among
men and become a brother of the race of Adam, would
have been astounded at the thought of such a condescension of love. He would have asked himself whether it was

possible, that the pure and simple infinity of God's perfections should take a human nature with all its limitations
and inevitable imperfections. If he were convinced that
this astounding thing was to come to pass, and were bidden
to conceive in what manner God would come among men,
he would no doubt have imagined an advent of tremendous power and majesty, in which the Godmade man
Who was of necessity King and Master of the world in
His own right, would descend from heaven in all the
splendor of His kingship, compelling the hearts of men
to adore Him and to love Him by the very splendor of
His majesty and the power of His human glory.

The Winner of Hearts

But the ways of God are not our ways, and His
thoughts are not our thoughts. He wishes from mankind
the love and devotion of hearts and the willing service,
which springs from love, not the compelled and cowering
submission which He could so easily enforce and which
would be so worthless to Him. By some unfathomable
mystery of His own exceeding goodness, God loves each
of us with a personal love and He has an infinite desire
to receive the love of our hearts in return. Therefore,
when the Son of God became man, when the Word was
made Flesh in order that He might dwell amongst us, He
came not to compel but to win our hearts. He appeared
amongst us in such a guise as to reveal to us the love and
yearning of God for our affection and the kindness and

[113]

the lovableness of God whereby He is infinitely worthy in Himself of all our love.

Viewed in this light, the babyhood, the childhood, and the youth of Christ are so clear and beautiful a mirror of God's lovableness, that many lifetimes would not be enough to exhaust their charming revelations of God's amiableness. In the mirror of the Word made Flesh, we can behold that infinite Lover, that God infinitely to be loved, Who, by disguising Himself in our flesh, has become visible to our very eyes, and Who by refusing to compel our love, has irresistibly taken captive the hearts of millions of the noblest and purest of mankind.

Consider the scene at Bethlehem, when the Incarnate Son of God was for the first time revealed to human eyes. All the history of the ages converges to that supreme moment of the birth of Christ. All after history of Christendom looks back upon that instant with adoring eyes. Yet, how lowly, how simple, and how touching is the advent of Christ into the midst of His brethren! He comes in the most gentle, the most appealing, the most loving guise which human nature could afford Him, the form of a new-born babe. In all the range of intelligent beings, there is no greater antithesis to the majesty, the power, the wisdom, the sufficiency, and the comprehension of the infinite God, than a new-born human babe.

As a Little Child

The sight of a little child in its helplessness and innocence, its dependence and its trustfulness, moves our hearts with an irresistible impulse of affection and protection. Under no other form could Jesus so easily gain entrance into the hearts of men as by becoming little, weak, and poor, wooing our hearts as a little babe. Looking at the manger at Bethlehem, dwelling upon the mystery of the endless God become a human child, the intelligence of man reels and staggers into ever-new comprehensions of the true nature of God's love. That great woman, St. Teresa of Avila, whose splendid intelligence was illuminated by the extraordinary experiences of her mystical inward life, once declared, as we have remarked before, that the reason why it is hard for us to become friends with God is that our nature is so different from His.

Friendship requires some equality. It is wonderful to us, knowing as we do our own wretchedness and nothingness and understanding in some dim way the endless beauty and holiness of God, that God should really wish to have our friendship. That He should demand our obedience and allegiance, our thankfulness and service is not wonderful, because these things are due to Him in strict justice since He is the Creator of all things. But that Almighty God should really desire to be friends with us, to love us and be loved, to give us His good gifts and in return to receive all the devotion of our hearts, is a thing difficult of realization. The sight of the Infant Jesus compels us to acknowledge this truth, for why should God become a little babe unless He wished us to love Him? What else can we give to a God become a child, except the most devoted and adoring love?

MIRRORS OF GOD

In order that it might be possible for us to be friends with God, it was necessary that He should establish some sort of equality between ourselves and Him. Yet, this would have seemed to our human intelligences an impossible thing. What comparison could there be between the creature, sprung from nothing, and the infinite Creator, between the Eternal and the finite, between Him whose handiwork we are and us the work of His hands? It required the infinite power and, if we may say so, the infinite ingenuity of God to overcome such an obstacle, to bridge over such an infinite chasm between the essential Being and essential nothingness. Yet God, with one gesture of His omnipotence, accomplished this inconceivable thing in a way most simple and effective. He bade His own Son, coequal with Himself in all eternity, to assume our nature and to come to us as a little human child, stretching His arms wide in an universal gesture of love and friendliness in the manger of Bethlehem, as He was later on to open them to embrace the whole world from the saving wood of the cross.

For the Lowliest

By this stupendous wonder, God has made it possible for the least and lowliest of us to be friends with Him. For who is there so weak, so lowly, so simple, that he cannot befriend a little babe? God has become a man, a child, and by that fact has made it possible that all men should be His friends. He has put Himself on a plane of equality not only with the greatest and most intelligent, but with the simplest and lowliest of His human brethren.

We have become too much accustomed to this sublime and moving spectacle. How is it that the sight of the infant Jesus does not utterly melt and conquer our stony hearts? Do we realize that this Child, cold, weak, poor, born in a stable, cradled in a manger, with only the adoring presence of Mary and of Joseph for all His court, is the King of kings, the Lord of lords, supreme God of heaven and earth, the Ruler of the whole universe, the infinitely happy, sufficient unto Himself in all things? It is told of St. Francis of Assisi, that when he had prepared the first Christmas crib, he had put into the manger the statue of the Infant Jesus, and after gathering his brethren about to show them this visible representation of God's infinite and condescending love, he spent the entire night weeping tears of love and gratitude, repeating over and over again one saying, which synopsized the stupendous meaning of that spectacle, "So great a God, so tiny a babe." So great a Majesty, so appealing a littleness, so infinite a power, so lowly a weakness, so stupendous a God-head, so gentle and little a child!

"GREAT LITTLE ONE!"

Crashaw, that fiery poet whose quaint syllables burn and thrill with the love of God, cries out in an ecstasy of poetic realization:

"Welcome all wonders in one sight!
Eternity shut in a span!
Summer in winter! day in night!

[117]

Heaven in earth! and God in man!
Great little One, whose all-embracing birth
Lifts earth to Heaven, stoops Heaven to earth!"

The whole story of the youth of Christ, as it is preserved for us in Christian tradition and in the priceless record of the Scriptures, continues this resistless appeal of the Incarnate God for our friendship and our love. The youth of Christ, like His infancy, mirrors for us with wonderful clearness the strength and tenderness of God's uncreated love for all mankind. Every episode of Christ's youth reveals to us more and more of the condescension, the affection, and the lowliness of our Savior. Christ had every characteristic needed to win the pure love of noble and devoted hearts. He is the one perfect Man of history, the one in Whom even His enemies could find no spot nor stain. Even those who fiercely oppose His teachings and refuse to believe the message of infinite love, which He came to bring to earth, must acknowledge Him as the greatest of all mankind, the truest Hero of all ages, the sublimest and most self-forgetful Friend and Benefactor to the human kind. Early in His youth these traits of the character of Christ shine forth from the pages of the Scriptures with appealing beauty.

IMMORTAL MEMORIES

We see Him cradled in the manger, borne in His mother's arms, receiving the homage of the shepherds and the magi, carried to be presented at the temple, submitting to the painful rite of circumcision, fleeing before the wrath

[118]

of Herod, entering into exile in Egypt, returning in obedience to His parents, taking up His abode in the obscure city of Nazareth, abiding in the temple in submission to His Father's will while His mother and St. Joseph sought Him sorrowing, dwelling at Nazareth in the poor house of the carpenter, earning His living by rude manual toil in the sweat of His brow in obedience to Mary and Joseph, He Who even according to human dignity was a prince of the house of David and Who in the eyes of heaven was the only Begotten Son of God made Man.

Christian art, the imaginations of poets, the sweet meditations of the Saints, and the quiet and loving thoughts of hundreds of millions of simple folk, lovers and followers of Christ, have dwelt upon these tender and moving episodes of His youth, drinking from them as from deep, healthful, cool-flowing springs, the waters of piety, of faith, of confidence, and of devoted and ever-growing love of God. They flow forth in an inexhaustible tide of consolation and of sweetness. From the earliest ages of the Christian Church, this touching story of the gospel has thrilled and moved the hearts of Christ's followers and until the end of time it will continue to stir each successive generation to a greater love of God.

All Ages Sanctified

If Christ had come into the world as a man in the full vigor of His powers, which He might easily have done, He might indeed have astounded mankind with the unique wonder of such a coming. But He had chosen, rather, to win our hearts by coming as a little Babe, growing through all the ages of youth as we have passed through them, making Himself like unto us in all things, except only sin which could not coexist with His divinity. Thus He has beautified and sanctified every successive age of human life. He has made infancy doubly dear because any child in its mother's arms reminds us of Jesus in the arms of Mary. He has made childhood beautiful beyond its natural beauty, because every child recalls to us the boy Jesus, Who is also the only-begotten of the Father, passing through every age of life to sanctify and bless it.

Family life, the home, the tender relations of child to mother and mother to child are blessed and made indescribably more holy by this presence of Christ in the midst of His family at Nazareth, the boy of the household, subject to His parents, giving to His mother such a filial devotion as never was before nor will be again on earth, cherishing His foster-father, St. Joseph, with that devoted love and duty which is a model for the actions of all children toward their fathers until the end of time.

Indeed, so familiar and so kind are the dealings of Christ with us, so natural, to use the word, are His actions, so much does He make Himself a part of our human life and existence, that we are in danger of overlooking something of the sublime revelation of God's love and lovableness which we may here gain by the contemplation of the Word made Flesh. This Babe, who lies in the manger, this Child, who looks upon us with such trustful and loving eyes, this Boy, bearing for our sake the dangers and tribulations of exile, this Youth, toiling and sweating in the rude work of His foster-father's shop is like us, yet He differs from us indescribably. He is one of us, yet infinitely above us. He is the Ambassador of the triune God, the only begotten Son of the Father, the equal of the Father and the Holy Ghost in all eternity, become man that He might convince us of God's love, that He might persuade us of God's lovableness, that He might enable us to become friends of God, that He might live and die in privation and sorrow, disappointments and anguish, in order to open to us the gates of heaven and bring us to share with Him forever the delights of His Father's kingdom.

From Christ's Eyes

From the eyes of Christ looks forth the person of the Son of God. He has a human nature, indeed, but there is no human person in Christ. The Person Who has assumed that human nature is in very deed and truth God Himself. The hands which Christ raises in blessing are the very hands of God. The Heart which throbs in pity for our sorrows, which pulses with love for us, and which prays with unwearying fervor for our happiness and salvation is the very Heart of God. The Feet, which walked the strange ways of earthly exile, are the Feet of Him Whose footsteps wear down the immemorial hills. The Arms, which toiled for us in the rudest and most wearisome labor, are the Arms of Him Who has balanced the stars in their courses and Who sustains the foundations of the deep. Let us be wise and prudent, and look often and thoughtfully upon the lovely mirror of God which is held up to us in the childhood and the youth of Christ. Let us pray that no gleam of heavenly beauty, no hint of the lineaments of God which this fair mirror may reveal to us may be lost to our souls. To know God and to love Him is the supreme purpose of our human nature. Let us contemplate Him in the mirror of Christ's youth.

CHAPTER X

THE MIRROR OF CHRIST'S MANHOOD

WE KNOW that God is the uncreated and infinite Goodness, that He is perfect in all things, and that He is therefore infinitely loving and infinitely lovable. He exists by virtue of His own essence. It is His nature to exist and, therefore, His being is without any limitations and His perfection is without any bounds. Whatever is in itself lovable, perfect and holy, and does not involve any imperfection can be said of God with absolute certainty. Hence even by the light of reason, we may know many things concerning the lovingness and the lovableness of the Most High.

If we could see God as He is and know Him as He is, His very beauty and amiability would ravish our hearts with love to such an extent that we could not help loving Him consumedly with all our hearts. In fact, the saints and angels in heaven who see God as He is in the beatific vision love Him of necessity and to the utmost extent of the capacity of their being. They cannot help loving God, nor can they help loving Him as much as is possible to them, because His goodness is so absolute and His lovableness so perfect that the will, whose object is good and which is attracted by good, finds itself carried away in the presence of this perfect and infinite Goodness. The human heart was made to love God; it craves after goodness with an irresistible longing; it desires happiness with a desire which is insatiable until it comes into the possession of God.

KNOWLEDGE AND LOVE

For this reason, to know God is to love Him. One great cause of our not loving God more is that we do not know Him well enough as He is. Though we may reason and convince ourselves of the goodness and lovableness of God, still we do not realize that Infinite Amiability. We need more help and encouragement to love God as we should, and we require further aids to appreciate how lovable is the Eternal Creator of our being.

God has revealed His goodness and amiability to us, let us repeat, not only in the vast book of nature, but in the supernatural revelations of the old and the New Testament. Heroes and heroines of the Old Testament —their lives sublime proofs of God's power—are recorded in the historic and prophetic books of the old law. All these are so many revelations of God's lovableness. His goodness and His power, His tender concern for the salvation of mankind, His mercy in forgiving sins and His justice in avenging them, His patience and forgiveness, His splendid rewarding of the services of His friends and His swift confounding of the plans of His enemies are to the reverent and thoughtful mind, but so many more revelations of His lovableness and so many more reasons for loving God.

It is in the New Testament, as we have said, that the

character of Christ and of those who surround Him as His disciples and apostles hold up before us a mirror of God's excellence, amiability, and beauty, incomparably greater than the witness of nature, the course of human history, or even the splendid and moving story of the old law and of the primitive history of mankind. We have seen how the mirror of Christ's infancy and youth reveals to us more of the divine goodness and condescension than was ever elsewhere vouchsafed to mankind. Let us now consider the manhood of that perfect Model of all holiness and let us see what thoughts of the amiability of the Most High will come to us from the memory of the gospel story.

THE WORD MADE FLESH

Reading the simple, moving pages of the gospel in which Christ's followers have set down their inspired memories of His words and actions and of the sayings and deeds of those who surrounded Him, we are impressed from the very beginning by the exceeding sweetness, kindness, and amiability of the Word made Flesh. As the infant Jesus lay in the manger, He summoned to Him first of all, and by the message of an Angel, the simplest, poorest, lowliest folk who dwelt on the hillsides of Judea near the bleak stable in which that heavenly child was born. The shepherds, watching over their flocks, heard the first tidings of the coming of the new-born King. "And there were in the same country shepherds watching, and keeping the night-watch over their flock.

"And behold an Angel of the Lord stood by them, and the brightness of God shone round about them, and they feared with a great fear.

"And the Angel said to them: 'Fear not; for, behold, I bring you good tidings of great joy, that shall be to all the people;

" 'For: This day is born to you a Savior, Who is Christ the Lord, in the city of David.

" 'And this shall be a sign unto you: You shall find the infant wrapped in swaddling clothes, and laid in a manger.'

"And suddenly there was with the Angel a multitude of the heavenly army, praising God, and saying:

" 'Glory to God in the highest; and on earth peace to men of good will' " (St. Luke ii. 8-14).

To the Lowly and Poor

It was to the lowly and the poor that Christ first announced His coming, and this love of His for the humble and the simple of the world is shown throughout His life on earth. He was born of the Virgin Mary, who was descended, it is true, from the house of David, but who was a lowly maiden of Israel. Unknown to the princes of the temple, unheeded by the proud men, and women who counted themselves the arbiters of the destiny of the Jewish nation, she lived obscurely, a life of laborious toil, of patient prayer, in the midst of the poor, in one of the most forgotten and hidden villages of the despised nation of the Jews. No wonder then, that when the time was come, according to the will of His Father, for Him to leave His dear mother and His peaceful home and go to preach salvation to the chosen people, He continued the same loving preference for the needy and the forgotten as had characterized His whole life on earth.

It might have seemed to our human wisdom that the best method for Christ to begin His career of preaching and teaching would have been to proceed at once to Jerusalem, the capital of His nation, where dwelt the Scribes and Pharisees, the chief Priests and the Roman Governor, whose iron hand held sway over the chosen people of God. There Christ, had He wished to do so, would have been able easily to ingratiate Himself with those who held power over His people. He could have astounded them by the wonder of His miracles, healed their diseases and afflictions, and convinced them by His masterly eloquence and the sublime power of His intellect that He was indeed the Son of God and the Savior of Israel. Yet, He kept aloof from the great and mighty of this earth and consorted with the humble and the poor. From the shores of Lake Genesareth He chose twelve humble fishermen to be His apostles and the future princes of that spiritual kingdom which He was come to establish on earth. He walked through the towns and over the dusty highways of Judea, calling about Him the multitudes of the common people, with their wounds and diseases, their rude manners, their thoughtless pressing and crowding about Him, their greediness for the miraculous loaves multiplied by His bounty, and their indifference and carelessness concerning the Word of God.

[127]

COMPASSION ON THE MULTITUDE

He never wearied of teaching, consoling, and healing the multitudes of the poor. The very apostles themselves, who had sprung from the lowliest of the lowly, grew weary time and again of the importunities of the multitude. Christ never repelled them, never ceased His beneficent ministrations in their favor. When the throngs of lame and blind pressed about Him, guided by their eager relatives, He laid His hand on them and healed them. When the lepers cried out to Him from afar, exposing to Him their loathsome forms, eaten and disfigured by that dread disease, He bade them be clean. When the man who had been ailing thirty years, stricken by the palsy, told Him of his sorrow when the waters of the pond of Probatica were troubled by the Angel and he had no one to put him in the pond that he might be healed, Jesus said to him, "Arise, take up thy bed and walk." And immediately the man was made whole and he took up his bed and walked (St. Luke ii. 9-11).

Then the sorrowful mother of Naim came weeping to the gate of the city, following her dead son, "The only son of his mother; and she was a widow; and a great multitude of the city was with her, Whom when the Lord had seen, being moved with mercy toward her, He said to her: 'Weep not.' And He came near and touched the bier. And they that carried it stood still. And he said: 'Young man, I say to thee, arise.' And he that was dead, sat up,

and began to speak. And He gave him to his mother"
(St. Luke vii. 12-15).

THE MIRACLES OF MERCY

"And there was a certain woman having an issue of
blood, twelve years, who had bestowed all her substance on
physicians and could not be healed by any. She came behind Him, and touched the hem of His garments; and
immediately the issue of her blood stopped.

"And Jesus said: 'Who is it that touched me?' And
all denying, Peter and they that were with him said:
'Master, the multitudes throng and press Thee, and dost
thou say, "Who touched Me?" '

"And Jesus said: 'Somebody hath touched Me; for I
know that virtue is gone out from me.'

"And the woman seeing that she was not hid, came
trembling, and fell down before His feet, and declared
before all the people for what cause she had touched Him,
and how she was immediately healed.

"But He said to her: 'Daughter, thy faith hath made
thee whole; go thy way in peace' " (St. Luke viii. 43-48).

When the Ruler of the synagogue came to Him, Jairus,
whose daughter was dying, He went to his home and al-
though they found the daughter dead, He raised her up
to life again and restored her to the astonished parents.
The universal pity of Christ and His unfailing compassion
and response to the prayers of the unfortunate and the
afflicted give us some notion of the endless pity of God,
Who has compassion on all the works of His hands, Who

hears our slightest prayer, and grants us far more than we deserve to receive for our petitions. In the sacred humanity of Christ, the lovableness of God is made visible and His beneficence comes home to us. We can conjecture from these acts of tenderness and healing which we see, the endless series of God's beneficences which we know upon the secure word of faith.

THE LOVE OF THE PEOPLE

The actions of those about Jesus teach us also the wonderful lovableness of His character. The multitudes follow Him everywhere. They crowd upon Him day and night. When He goes out into the desert, they throng after Him, forgetting even to make any provision for their food, so that His merciful Heart is fain to multiply the loaves and the fishes, working a great miracle in order that they may not go away fasting. The story of St. Matthew concerning those touching episodes brings home to us anew how worthy to be loved is the God-man for His compassion on our human weaknesses. The first episode occurs after Jesus has received the sad news of the beheading of St. John the Baptist in prison. His disciples when they had buried the body of St. John "came and told Jesus."

"Which when Jesus had heard, he retired from thence by a boat, into a desert place apart, and the multitudes having heard of it, followed Him on foot out of the cities.

"And He coming forth saw a great multitude, and had compassion on them, and healed their sick.

"And when it was evening, His disciples came to Him,

saying: 'This is a desert place, and the hour is now passed: send away the multitudes, that going into the towns, they may buy themselves victuals.'

"But Jesus said to them, 'They have no need to go: give you them to eat.'

"They answered Him: 'We have not here, but five loaves, and two fishes.'

"Who said to them: 'Bring them hither to Me.'

"And when He had commanded the multitude to sit down upon the grass, He took the five loaves and the two fishes, and looking up to heaven, He blessed, and broke, and gave the loaves to His disciples, and the disciples to the multitudes.

"And they did all eat, and were filled. And they took up what remained, twelve full baskets of fragments.

"And the number of them that did eat, was five thousand men, besides women and children" (St. Matthew xiv. 13-22).

ANOTHER KINDLY MIRACLE

The second incident related in the next chapter of St. Matthew is very like the first. Again, "there came to Him great multitudes, having with them the dumb, the blind, the lame, the maimed, and many others: and they cast them down at His feet and He healed them. And Jesus called together His disciples and said: 'I have compassion on the multitude, because they continue with me now three days, and have not what to eat, and I will not send them away fasting lest they faint in the way'" (St. Matthew

xvi. 30-32). Again, He multiplied the loaves and the fishes which His disciples had with them, and when four thousand men besides children and women, had eaten their fill, they took up seven baskets-full of what remained of the fragments. Of what other leader or teacher was it ever truly said that the multitudes followed him for three days fasting? Or who else in the history of the world was ever able to feed his friends by the miraculous multiplication of food performed by his own power?

How gentle and patient He is with all men. His own apostles tried Him often by their lack of comprehension of His teachings. The proud Scribes and Pharisees persecuted Him and sought to stir the people up against Him. The multitudes, whom He had healed of their diseases and cleansed of their sins, often showed little gratitude for His manifold favors. Yet, nowhere does He manifest the least impatience, nowhere is He harsh or severe. He carries out, always and to the letter, the prediction of the prophet that He should not break the bruised reed nor extinguish the smoking flax.

A MAN ENTIRELY GODLIKE

Only when He denounces the hypocrisy and hardheartedness of the Scribes and Pharisees do His words flame with a righteous anger. This anger is in condemnation of their pride and stubbornness; not bitter anger, but just and holy. The perfection of the character of Christ is so absolute that the claim of His followers that He is truly the Son of God, co-equal with the Eternal Father in all eternity, is justified by the simple narrative of His words and deeds. It is a hard saying for the race of men to be bidden to bow down and adore as God one of their own flesh and blood, like unto themselves in all things except sin. According to the belief of some of the Fathers, it was this command to adore in anticipation the sacred humanity of the Son of God which was the occasion of the rebellion of the evil angels. It is certain that if the life and actions of Christ had not been entirely Godlike, the critical and skeptical generations of our day would never have continued as they do to the hundreds of millions to adore Him as the true Son of God, truly made man. Christ's life was so divine, His character so Godlike, His compassion so perfect, His innocence so exquisite, His wisdom so heavenly, His patience so sublime, His love so great, and His zeal so burning, that we cry out with the centurion, "Indeed this Man was the Son of God" (St. Mark xvi. 39).

Our Blessed Lot

How blessed are we whose lot has fallen in days which follow the Incarnation of the Son of God! Even the Jews of the Old Testament, prophets, sages, judges, and kings of Israel knew only dimly the great mercy and lovableness of God compared to the floods of comprehension which stream upon our minds from the contemplation of the Word made Flesh. They knew God in vision and prophecy; they were shown His power and greatness by signs and wonders, and were helped by His grace to read the great book of nature and to sing, as David sang, the majesty and splendor of the God-head from the tremendous spectacle of the storm, from the glowing of the stars in tranquil heavens, from the depths of oceans and the heights of air. But it remained for us to know God in the flesh, to watch His human actions with human eyes, and to become acquainted with the lineaments of His divinity, mirrored in the perfections of the humanity which He had assumed for all ages, taking flesh from the most pure virgin Mary that the Word might dwell amongst us, a blood-brother of our own race.

"Come to Me!"

Christ in the prime of His manhood, having grown in wisdom and age and grace before God and men to the full stature of His perfect humanity, will be forever to our human race the brightest and most excellent mirror of God's inscrutable perfections, the surest proof of God's infinite lovableness, and the most convincing evidence of His boundless love for man. We have now a human Heart which is also the Heart of God beating for us and pleading for us forever to His Father. That same Heart, with the tender affection of Christ's humanity for us, pleads likewise with our hearts, with a most insistent desire that We should love Him and love His heavenly Father with all the devotion of which our being is capable. To love Christ is to love God; to know Christ is to know God; to have the friendship of Christ is to have the friendship of God. "All things are delivered to Me by My Father. And

"The dying Christ is the sublimest mirror of the love of God for man."

(Christ on the Cross by Velasquez)

no one knoweth the Son but the Father; neither doth anyone know the Father but the Son, and He to Whom it
shall please the Son, to reveal Him. Come to Me, all you
that labor, and are burdened, and I will refresh you. Take
up My yoke upon you, and learn of Me because I am
meek and humble of heart: And you shall find rest to your
souls. For My yoke is sweet and My burden is light" (St.
Matthew xi. 27-30).

CHAPTER XI

THE MIRROR OF CHRIST'S PASSION

IT IS midday on Calvary, the noon of the first Good Friday. Three sombre crosses, the symbols of infamy and the instruments of the most shameful punishment known to the Roman law, stand out with terrible distinctness against the overcast sky. The gloom of the heavens, preternatural and awful, is yet not so deep as to obscure the tremendous spectacle on yonder fated hill of expiation. As we hurry towards the scene of the crucifixion, we behold the three agonized figures, raised aloft on the crosses, their limbs writhing in anguish, their figures darkly outlined against the frowning heavens.

The crowds at the foot of the crosses and scattered all about in a wide circle are hushed and terrified. They have been loud and clamorous before, shouting insults and ridicule at the still Figure in the center and bidding Him in derision, "If Thou be the Son of God, come down from the cross and we will believe Thee!" (St. Matthew xxviii. 40). But the superhuman patience and sweetness of that willing victim, the Godlike dignity of His bearing, even on this infamous gibbet, the sight of the strange disturbances of nature which gradually increase with the progress of His agony, all these have hushed the loud clamors of the crowd. They have been waiting there for

[136]

nearly three hours to see the end of this agony, and the sight of so much suffering, so calmly and willingly borne, is beginning to move the hearts of many. Then, too, whenever they look up into the agonized Face some of them, whose souls are not altogether hardened, see there an expression which stirs the best instincts of their nature and makes them anxious and sad. For on that sad Countenance, disfigured with blood and dust, there is an expression of such agonized love. It seems as though this Man were dying less of the intense and awful physical and mental sufferings which they have heaped upon Him than of His own immense yearning and the unbearable love which He has for all mankind, even for His executioners.

THE AMAZING PRAYER

The words which He has uttered, gasped out with such terrible effort from a bosom drained of its blood and strength and fixed in the strained and painful attitude of crucifixion, have spoken of a love and a self-forgetfulness so sublime as to be appalling. Scarcely had He been lifted up, His limbs scored with the scourges and torn with stones where He had fallen on the way to Calvary, His hands and Feet pouring blood, the crown of thorns piercing His brow and staining His countenance with red streams of anguish, scarcely was this moving spectacle shown clearly to the whole gathering when they heard Him utter a prayer of forgiving love for His very executioners!

"Father," He had cried out, and the words rang with anguished supplication up to the skies, "Father, forgive

[137]

them for they know not what they do!" (St. Luke xxiii. 34). Had His first thought been one of love for the very men who had so brutally done Him to death, the Scribes and Pharisees by their pitiless houndings, the soldiers by their brutal carrying out of the sentence of crucifixion? What a strange and unusual prayer for a condemned and dying man to utter! If He had prayed for vengeance, they would have thought it natural. If He had prayed for death to release Him from such sufferings, they would have considered that He was wise to wish for death. But He had prayed for His executioners! The more thoughtful among them pondered on that prayer as they saw Him dying.

The Figure on the Cross

Through a silent and weary multitude we push our way in pious imagination to gain the foot of the cross and to contemplate our dying Friend, the supreme Lover of mankind. With difficulty we thread a path through the crowd and stand at the foot of the cross. To the dying thieves, one at either side, we hardly give a glance. Like a magnet, the Figure on the cross in the midst draws and holds our straining eyes.

How familiar is that Figure today, over all the world. There are many images of Christ in many churches and in many pious homes. Great artists have used their sublimest skill to delineate the calm and majestic beauty of the fairest and strongest of the sons of men. But the Figure of Christ on the cross, suffering and dying for the love of mankind, is the most impressive and characteristic of all representations of the God Man. The cross is no more the symbol of shame, but a glorious sign of sufferings borne for the love of mankind.

Let us look upon the Crucified, therefore, as we stand at the foot of the cross, beside Mary His mother, and St. John, and those holy women who completed the small group of His friends. Let us look at His dying agony and try earnestly to learn the lesson of love which He gives us from His cross. It is worth all the riches of the world, all the science of earth, all happiness and power to learn that one lesson. Indeed, to gain one degree more of the real love of Christ from the contemplation of His surpassing love for us is worth more than the whole material universe.

CHRIST'S SUFFERINGS

The physical and mental agony of our Savior wound the heart to behold them. He is suffering as never before did man suffer, as mortal never shall suffer again. The gaping wounds, the streaming blood, and the paleness of utter exhaustion which we see as we look upward at the Crucified give us some faint notion of the bodily anguish which He endures. His whole constitution, His nervous system, and His sensibility to pain are the most perfect and delicate, for He chose His own body and made it a perfect instrument for the most exquisite and voluntary suffering.

But the inward anguish of His memory, His intellect, and His will are more agonizing than these bodily pains.

[139]

All the loathsome sins of the earth, from the first sin of Eve until the last offense of the end of human history are present to Him, and He bears their foulness, their wickedness, the perfectly comprehended horror of their shame. He has become sin personified and He is God incarnate! Here, on the cross, the extremes of creation meet, and the Son of God conquers sin indeed forever, but at a cost proportionate to that immense victory. The bitterness and anguish of that awful struggle lacerate the heart and soul of the Victim with far more pain than the whips of the soldiers, the stones on the way, the nails and splinters of the cross, and the crown of thorns had inflicted on His sensitive body. For three hours He has hung there, lifted up between heaven and earth, a very image and embodiment of the greatest agony of body and of mind. What is the meaning of such extreme suffering?

THE SUBLIMEST MIRROR OF LOVE

It is an expression of His immense and personal love for you. The dying Christ is the sublimest mirror of the love of God for man. Look into His face as you stand at the foot of the cross, and you shall read in His eyes, fixed on you with dying intentness, the most singular love for you. He loves you in particular; He suffers and He dies for you as though there were no one else in the world to be redeemed. So great and self-immolating is His love for you that He would endure all this torment willingly for you alone. Indeed, He does endure it for you as though there were no other sinner in the world to be won to His love save only you.

We have to struggle to bring home this truth to our hearts, because though it is most sure, it is so amazing as to stun our powers of realization. There have been, to be sure, many followers of Christ who have lived long lives in His service, done many works in His name, and died without any adequate realization of His love for them. Yet, unless we realize this truth and bring it home to ourselves, we shall miss a very wonderful help to increase in the love of God. For love begets love, and we can hardly realize the immense and personal love of Christ for us without loving Him devotedly in return.

"How He Loves Me!"

Look up, then, into the eyes of the dying Christ, and repeat over and over again to yourself, "He loves me! He is dying for me! He dies for me out of the greatness of His love! These sufferings, this agony and His blood and tears are signs, not only of the greatness of my sins, but of the immensity of His love for me. He wishes me for His friend and He is willing to pay even this price for my love. Indeed, He would not have needed to offer such a terrible atonement to win pardon for me from His heavenly Father, but it is necessary that He should suffer thus to melt my heart and to make me understand how He loves me."

Since Christ is as truly God as He is truly man, every one of His actions has a limitless value in His Father's sight. The least prayer offered up by Him would have been enough to redeem any number of worlds. The least drop of His blood, as St. Thomas Aquinas says in his Eucharistic hymn, would have sufficed to wash the whole world clean of sin. It was not necessary for our salvation that Christ should have suffered all these things. He might have merely showed Himself on earth, have offered up one all-powerful prayer for our salvation, and then have returned to heaven without having felt anything of our mortal sufferings.

The Wooing of Hearts

This would have been enough for our redemption, but not enough to satisfy His love nor to have persuaded our dull hearts to love Him. Even after all He has done for us, so many of us, even of His friends, remain cold and and unresponsive to His affection for us. What more could He have done to win our love? He Who is Eternal, has wooed our hearts from the manger at Bethlehem where He became weak and small for our love, from the toils of His foster father's workshop where He labored and suffered for us, from the weary highroads and byways of Israel where He preached and worked miracles for us, from the Last Supper where He spoke to us most movingly of His love. But now, on the cross, He sums up and confirms forever the testimony of His own immense love, by dying for us. "Greater love than this," He has said, "no man hath, that a man lay down his life for his friend" (St. John xv. 13). He was never satisfied with all His other proofs of love until He had crowned them by the supreme proof of dying for us. As you look upon Him on the cross, He Who could have chosen any other manner of leaving this world, even the most glorious, ask yourself, "How much He must love me, if He deliberately chose to die like this to show me His love!"

THE VICTORY OF LOVE

If we once realize this, our heart cannot resist His appeal. Such a love cannot fail, if it is understood, to arouse an answering love. The eyes of Christ, dying for us on the cross, can kindle love in our soul. It was this that stirred the saints to such transports of self-forgetting love that they did things which to us are strange and singular. But they are natural and logical as a return for so much love as Christ shows us on His cross. Unable by ordinary means to express the love which such love kindled in their own bosoms, the saints longed to suffer and to die to show their love. They willingly gave up all pleasures, for they did not wish to live pleasantly and comfortably when their Savior had chosen for their sake to die on the cross. The ordinary preferences of the human heart were reversed for them. They loved what the world fears—hardships, sufferings, dishonor, because these made them more like Christ and gave them an opportunity to show their love to Him. They shunned what the world most craves for and strives to gain, as wealth, honor, ease, freedom from pain, and the enjoyment of delights, because all these things made them unlike Christ, dying for them, out

[143]

of love for them, on the hard, dishonorable, destitute, and pitiful gibbet to which He was fixed by His great love.

A Prayer for Love

Look up again into Christ's loving countenance, gazing down at you with a look of pleading and affection, as He dies for love of you. Say to Him, again and again, with all the earnestness and sincerity you can command, "My God, made man for me, crucified for me, I love You. I love You with all my heart, as You have loved me with all Your heart. I love You for Your own sake, because You are so good in Yourself, because You are endlessly worthy of all my love. By the power of Your sacred wounds, make me love You more and more. By the might of Your blood, which is worth a million worlds of souls, kindle Yourself in my heart the love which You wish me to have for You. By the flame of Your love, consuming Your Heart, light in my heart the inextinguishable burnings of a mighty love for You.

"You can love me as much as You desire, because Your love is in Your own control. You can love me even though I am so undeserving of love. But I cannot love You without Your aid, even though You are so perfectly and endlessly amiable.

"If it is good for me to be loved by You, O incarnate Truth, the Only Begotten of God the Father from eternity, it is better for me to love You in return, to the limit of my powers, to the extent of my capacity for love. You only can realize in me by Your grace, Your inspiration, the constant help of Your omnipotence, the power that I have to love You. Let me put no obstacles in the way of that love in my heart. As You overcame all obstacles to Your own love for me, leaping over the chasm which yawns betwixt finiteness and eternity so as to become a man like me, taking passable flesh so that You could suffer and die for me, so also overcome all the obstacles that prevent me from loving You as I should.

"O Christ, Be Pitiful!"

"Let not the balance, O Lord, be too great against me. I have already to endure that I am by nature so limited and impotent in my power of loving that in the friendship which You wish to exist between us I shall always be far less able to love You than You can love me, even with Your human Heart. At least, in Your pitiful love, raise me to the extreme of self-forgetting love of You of which my small heart is capable.

"It would have been an agony for You, greater than that of Your passion, if You had not been able to suffer and die to redeem me. For me, it is an unbearable pain not to love You as I should love and wish to love. It was You, O Lord, who kindled the heart of Francis of Assisi until he rivaled the seraphs in their love. It was You Who inflamed the soul of Teresa of Avila until she sighed either to suffer or to die. It is You Who fan the flames of love in the bosoms of the saints on earth and in the angelic essences and the glorious souls in heaven.

"Be pitiful, O crucified Love, and give me more and

[145]

more lavishly of the love of You. You, Who have died for me, do not deny me the love which will make me live and die for You. It is the property of love, O merciful, O dying Christ, to exchange all good things with the one who is loved. The greatest of all goods, on earth and in heaven, is to love You mightily, purely, for Your own sake and because You Yourself are worthy of all love. Give me, truest of Lovers, I ask it by the greatness of Your love, this best of Your gifts!"

Finis.

OTHER BOOKS
BY REV. E. F. GARESCHE, S. J.

PROSE:

The following set of ten books may be purchased for $8.50 complete. Single copies, 90c. Postage extra.

Ever Timely Thoughts	The Values Everlasting
Life's Lessons	Your Interests Eternal
The Most Beloved Woman	Your Neighbor and You
The Paths of Goodness	Your Own Heart
The Things Immortal	Your Soul's Salvation

A Vade Mecum for Nurses and Social Workers............$1.00
Children of Mary (Talks to Sodalists)....................1.00
Communion With the Spirit World.......................1.50
God in His World—First Series..........................1.50
God in His World—Second Series........................1.50
Great Christian Artists (83 full-page illustrations in sepia)....3.50
Social Organization in Parishes..........................2.75
Sodality Conferences—First Series.......................2.75
Sodality Conferences—Second Series......................2.75
Sodality Manual..40
Sodalities for Nurses.....................................1.50
The Patient's Book..80
The Patient's Guide.......................................80
The Teachings of the Little Flower........................1.25
The Training of Writers...................................1.10
Training for Life...1.75
The Sacred Heart and the Catholic Home........(In Preparation)

POETRY:

The Four Gates...$1.50
The World and the Waters.................................1.50
To Margaret Mary in Heaven...............................50
War Mothers..60

PAMPHLETS:

A Month of Devotions to Mary, Patroness of Vocations......$0.10
Closed Retreats for Lay Folk..............................10
Novena to the Little Flower...............................15
Novena to the Little Flower (Polish Edition)..............15
Teaching for God...10

These books may be ordered through any bookseller.